THE STORY OF THE SANTAL

WITH AN ACCOUNT OF THE SANTAL REBELLION

JAMES MERRY MACPHAIL

GYAN

Published by

Gyan Publishing House
5, Ansari Road
Daryaganj, New Delhi-110002
Phone: 011-47034999, 9811692060
E-mail: books@gyanbooks.com

Distribution Network
gyanbooks.com
India, USA, Canada, UK, Australia

ISBN: 978-93-7097-216-2 (PB)

First Published, 1922

2nd Impression 2025

Printed at: Gyan Press, Delhi.

THE STORY OF THE SANTAL
Author: JAMES MERRY MACPHAIL

THE STORY OF THE SANTAL WITH AN ACCOUNT OF THE SANTAL REBELLION

JAMES MERRY MACPHAIL

1922

THE STORY OF THE SANTAL:

WITH AN ACCOUNT OF THE SANTAL REBELLION.

Introduction.

THE following papers appeared originally in *The Statesman* and are republished by kind permission of the Editor.

In them an attempt is made to depict the lives of two typical Santals, a man and a woman, from the cradle to the grave—it being understood, however, that the Santal has neither a cradle nor a grave. Manka and Maku are in one sense fictitious characters, but everything which is said of them is true; they are never represented as saying or doing anything which Santals have not said or done. As an occasional Santali word is inevitable it may be explained that the pronunciation follows the general rules which prevail in most of the Indian vernaculars. G is always hard, as in *gold* *Kh* is pronounced like two separate letters, as in *inkhorn*. As the Santals had no written language of their own, the Roman character was generally adopted by the missionaries who first studied it, although one of the earliest of them, Dr. Phillips of Orissa, used the Bengali letters for a Santali grammar which he published in 1834. The Roman character is now regarded as the most convenient, for the sounds for which it has no equivalents are peculiar to Santali, and in any case would have to be represented by diacritical signs. Of these sounds, those which first attract attention are what are described in English as the half-letters, and written k', c,' t,' and p.'. Skrefsrud, our chief authority on the Santali language, gives elaborate directions for their pronunciation:

c', for instance, is pronounced by sharply inhaling the breath, and suddenly closing the throat and at the same time striking with the flat of the tongue sharply against the palate and reopening it without allowing the breath to touch that organ. The directions for acquiring the other sounds are equally precise, but for popular purposes it may suffice to say that *k*,' *p*' and *t*' are pronounced as if one were going to say *k*, *p* and *t* but stopped short. Thus, *dak*' the Santali word for water, sounds as if the speaker had begun with the intention of saying *dak*, but "clipped" the final consonant. It is said that the only place outside of the Santal country where these sounds are to be heard is in Glasgow and some other places in the West of Scotland. When a Glasgow man says: "The fac' o' the ma'er is that on Sa'urday I'am gaun doun the wa'er," (the fact of the matter is that on Saturday I am going down the water), the *t* in 'Saturday' and 'water' is almost exactly like the Santali half *t*' and the *c* in 'fact' (with the terminal *t* dropped) is remarkably like the Santali half c'. Among the consonants there is a palatal *t*, *d*, and *r*, as well as a dental, as is common in India, and the former are printed with a dot underneath to distinguish them. *N* with a dot over it is pronounced like the English *ng* in ring. Thus *baṅ* the Santali word for "no", sounds *bang*. *Ń* with an acute accent is like the *ñ* in the Spanish *señor*. Thus *ńam*, to find or get, sounds something like *nyam*.

Of the nine million inhabitants of India now described as Animists the Santals are the largest tribe. In 1911 they numbered 2,178, 716. They used to be described as of the Kolarian group of aborigines, but more careful study of their skulls in recent years has led to the conclusion that they are typical examples of the pure Dravidian stock. The Santal country extends from Bhagalpur in the north to Orissa in the south, and large numbers of the tribe are now to be found in the tea districts of Darjeeling, the Dooars, and Assam. Recently, too, they have shown a tendency to migrate across the Ganges towards Dinajpur and Rangpur, to form permanent settlements in these districts. During the war thousands of Santals served the King as members of the Indian

Labour Corps, in France and Mesopotamia, in Baluchistan and on the North-West Frontier.

In Chapter III, there is a story, that of the Little Girl who always found Helpers, which is included in the collection of Santali Folk-lore published by the late Rev. Dr. Andrew Campbell; but the writer had obtained that story in the original from a Santal friend before Dr. Campbell's book appeared. It may be added that without Dr. Campbell's help these chapters could not have been written. On the second anniversary of his death, this book is affectionately dedicated to his memory.

J. M. M.

BAMDAH,

8th July, 1921.

THE STORY OF THE SANTAL:

WITH AN ACCOUNT OF THE SANTAL REBELLION.

CONTENTS.

THE STORY OF THE SANTAL:

WITH AN ACCOUNT OF THE SANTAL REBELLION.

CHAPTER I.

A SANTAL VILLAGE.

THE Santal village of Taletandi—the Plain of the Palmyra Palm—consisted of one long but by no means unlovely street in what was once a part of Birbhum, but now lies within the Santal Parganas. It consisted of about fifty huts, and as in suburban language they were all self-contained, none of them being even semi-detached, they formed a straggling row on each side of the street, fully half a mile long. Each hut was built of brown mud, which long exposure to summer suns had hardened till it was almost as firm as concrete, and thatched by a long grass which grew everywhere except where the land was ploughed or the cattle grazed. The house as a rule consisted of one apartment, but mud-built partitions furnished recesses when the family multiplied. There were no windows, and all the ventilation was through the door and the roof, which was black with soot. In building the walls, little niches had been left to serve as cupboards, and in one of these those who could afford a light at night—they were a small minority—placed the tiny earthen saucer in which a piece of cotton floated in castor oil. A bamboo, suspended from the roof by home-made rope, served for hanging clothes on, and in very few houses was there much furniture beyond a ricketty string-bed or charpoy. A good many articles, such as a reaping-hook or sickle, and a small axe for chopping firewood, were stuck into the thatch. In a narrow verandah formed by the overhanging eaves of the roof, with a mud floor slightly elevated from the ground, was a fire-place or *culha*, also built of mud, and in some of the larger houses a hand-mill for grinding Indian corn and other grain.

Each house was separated from the street by a courtyard, fenced with sticks and branches, which served as a public reception room. In the larger houses, cattle sheds were fenced off and roofed in on one side of this courtyard, and in another corner was a pig-stye, but in the smaller houses the goats and other animals shared the same apartment with their owners. In every courtyard there was a roughly-made wooden stand for the waterpots, which were religiously emptied and cleaned at least once a day. Another article in general use was a piece of a tree trunk hollowed out like a mortar, in which the rice was husked by being pounded with an iron-tipped wooden pestle. But in the larger houses the husking and grain cleaning was done by the *dhinki*, which stood in the verandah. It was worked by the foot, turning on an axle pounding the grain in a hole in the ground. Another structure confined to the houses of the comparatively well-to-do was the dovecot. It stood in the middle of the yard, elevated on two substantial tree-trunks, upon which a platform was built. This was roofed in and well supplied with broken waterpots. Thorn bushes were tied to the pillars, as a safeguard against prowling jackals, or the half-domesticated cat,—who, by the way, is in Santali called *pusi*. Under the eaves of the roof articles too big to go inside were deposited—a yoke for the bullocks, for example—and the wooden ploughshare stood in one corner, and a hoe in another. In those days, brass vessels were not so common among the Santals, and the place was littered with old leaf-plates and drinking-cups, all made from the *sal*. Earthen pots were used for cooking. An article more common then than now was a spinning-wheel, on which the women spun the cotton grown in the fields.

The second line of defence from publicity was the garden. In most cases it was skirted by a few horse-radish trees, whose leaves were held in much esteem as a pot-herb while the bark and root were prized as domestic medicines. A little plot of tobacco was to be found in many gardens, and in their proper season a few castor oil plants, a little Indian corn, giant pumpkins that were trained up over the roof, some pepper, one or two varieties of beans, brinjals, and other country vegetables. There was also a modest attempt at ornamental gardening by means of a few straggling flowers and shrubs, most of which, like the basil, were of some economic use as well.

In the grass-grown street there were three points of interest which served as common meeting-places for the people. First and foremost among these was the *manjhithan,* a shrine sacred to the spirits of the deceased village chiefs. It consisted of a raised mud platform, with a thatch roof, supported by five wooden pillars, one in the centre and one at each corner. At the foot of the central pillar were two roughly-carved pieces of wood daubed with red paint, each of which represented a dead *manjhi* or village chief. The fact that there were two showed that the headman of Taletandi had two predecessors, that his grand-father had founded the village. Here sacrifices were offered to the spirits of these dead potentates. Ram Manjhi, the present headman, lived close to the shrine of his ancestors. In every respect he was the biggest man in the village. He had the largest house and two wives.

Not far away, under a shady jack tree, was the oil press, another public institution. Its construction was on the simplest plan. Two heavy wooden logs, the contiguous surfaces of which had been levelled, were kept in position, one on the top of the other, by uprights which perforated them and were themselves firmly fixed in the ground. In the middle of the upper surface of the lower beam a circular groove was cut with an outlet at one side. When oil was to be expressed the fruit—castor oil, mustard, neem or mahua—was wrapped up in leaves and placed in the centre of this groove. The two beams were then tied together by strong ropes and pressure was exerted by twisting these round with a pole and also by leverage. The oil dripped through the outlet into a receptacle placed in position to receive it.

The third favourite "howf" was the smithy. The blacksmith was not a Santal but a *Kamar.* He called himself a Hindu, and had an altar to Mahadeo in his courtyard. He and his forefathers had been born among the Santals, and had lived among them all their lives and spoke the Santali language as their native tongue. But they never intermarried with them nor would they eat with them. In some of the other villages the blacksmiths were Kols, more nearly allied to the Santals, but still distinct. The anvil was a hard rock,and the forge was an ingenious contrivance of a very simple kind, but not so easy to describe. The furnace itself was just a slight hollow in the ground protected by a mud screen which was pierced by two pieces of bamboo. The other ends of these bamboos communicated with two drum-like structures. The drum heads were covered with leather, with a hole to let the air out and in, and each leather was tied by a string to a bamboo which, fixed at its other end in the ground, acted as a spring. A boy or girl, standing on the drums, lifted his or her heels alternately from the holes, and the recoil of the bamboos raised the leather and allowed air to enter the drums. By depressing the heels and closing the holes the air was driven through the bamboo pipes into the furnace. The blacksmith kept the villagers supplied with the implements of agriculture and the weapons of the chase, most of which he manufactured from the iron ore his women-folk gathered in the bed of a river in the form of a fine dust. A common method of payment was to give him the weight of the article he had made in rice.

Outside one of the houses was a bullock cart, the only one in the village. Its spokeless wheels had been hewn out of a solid block, and a fine banyan tree had been sacrificed for this object.

When the other villagers wished to bring home from the jungle logs too heavy to carry, they tied them to a yoke and made their bullocks drag them along the ground.

In the neighbourhood of the village there was a group of about twenty-five sal trees which formed the *jaher* or sacred grove. It was consecrated to the *bongas* or demon gods, each of whom was represented by a piece of quartz, marked with vermilion, at the foot of one of the trees. By name these spirits were *Jaherera, More Turui Ko* (which means "five or six"), *Maraṅ Buru* or the great spirit, *Gosaeera* and *Pargana Bonya*, of whom more anon.

Another place of importance was the threshing-floor or *kharai*. It was simply a level piece of land which had been smoothed down, beaten hard, and smeared with cowdung. During the harvest a rude hut of tree branches was put up, in which the farmer or one of his men kept watch upon the grain lying on the threshing-floor throughout the night. It was in such a hut that Boaz was spending the night when Ruth went to him at the threshing-floor near Bethlehem when the barley was being winnowed. A platform was erected on the threshing-floor for storing the straw well beyond the reach of the cattle, with a long stick run through the middle of it to prevent the wind from blowing it away. To build this *marom*, as it was called, trees were hewn down in the jungle. They happened to be *doka* trees (*Odina Wodier, Roxb*) and when set up as the pillars of the platform they took root and sprouted, and so served the same purpose year after year. A well-beaten path led to the spring in a corner of a rice-field whence the villagers drew their supplies of drinking water. There was a river not far off, about dry from December till June, but often a turbid torrent in the rains. In it the people bathed—those who *did* bathe, and when they were so inclined—and when the spring failed them, which was seldom, they could usually get water for domestic purposes by digging in the sand of the river bed.

The surrounding country was undulating. The little valleys had been dammed up and terraced and turned into rice-fields, and the higher land near the village was cleared of timber and used for the Indian corn and similar crops. The cattle were turned into the jungle, where when the grass failed there were plenty of young trees to feed on. Among the forest trees the *sal* was the most conspicuous (the Santals called it *sarjom* and held it as sacred), but there was a great variety of other kinds as well—banyans and peepuls, mango and jack, tamarind, mahua, palmyra palms, Indian cotton trees, the neem and the fig, the palas and the catechu, interspersed with graceful clumps of bamboo and many berry-bearing bushes upon which the Santal children fed with as great an avidity as the beasts and the birds.

Great masses of black rock here and there broke through the surface of the earth. The soil for the most part was dry and sandy, with a plentiful admixture of white quartz. The hills which could be discerned at a short distance were masses of rock, but were wooded to the summit. They rose to a height of 800 feet; on a clear day one could make out the outline of Paresnath, nearly 5,000 feet high.

Baghmara, so called because it marked a place where a tiger had been killed, was the nearest village to Taletandi, at the distance of about a mile. In the cold season, when the fields were bare and a good many of the trees leafless, it could be easily seen. Two other villages at a greater distance must be mentioned—Banadih or Bear village, and Loatola or Fig-tree district—the former because it was the residence of the *des manjhi*, Barka by name, who held authority over a circle of villages; the latter because it held still higher rank in the Santal patriarchal system as the home of the *pargana* or head chief of the district, Thakra by name, who was the High Court of Appeal from the decisions of the village *manjhi* and his superior the *des manjhi*.

It was in Taletandi, amid these surroundings, that our hero Manka first saw the light of day.

CHAPTER II.

THE NEW FRIEND.

EARLY one morning in October, a good many years ago, a young Santal, Budhu by name, came out of his house in Taletandi and sat down on the sunny side of the street. There was a yellow tinge on the ricefields now, and a foretaste of the cold weather in the morning air, and Budhu drew his cloth tightly round him as he squatted on his heels. An older Santal soon came along and, sitting down beside him, held out his hand. Budhu drew from the folds of his waist cloth two tiny bamboo boxes, one containing dried tobacco leaf, the other lime, placed a little of each in the palm of his companion's hand—which was stained dark brown with tobacco juice,—and took an equal quantity for himself. "Even the man who rides an elephant begs tobacco" is a proverb among the Santals. Both mixed the lime and tobacco together with great deliberation and chewed it for a time in silence. "What is your news, nephew?" the older man asked at last. Among the Santals a spade is called anything but a spade, and a man is almost never addressed by name. Relationship is universally assumed to avoid the necessity of doing so. "Well, uncle, a new friend has come," replied Budhu. A grunt from the older man was the response, followed after an interval by the question, "Does it carry on the head or the shoulder?" "On the shoulder," said Budhu, and the grunt this time was a little heartier, expressing satisfaction that another man child had been born in the village.

Budhu was the youngest son of Manka Manjhi, now a venerable white-haired old man, held in high esteem in the village. It was his delight to tell of the stirring times he had seen in his youth. In those old days the Santals had lived by raiding the lowlands once a year as regularly and as completely as they now reaped their crops. They did little else, besides hunting, the proceeds of each raid being sufficient to keep them in food and clothing for the rest of the year. Old Manka remembered the great Cleveland Saheb, the Collector of Bhagalpur, who had exercised a unique influence for good over the hill tribes, ruling them on the "no police" system with the help of their own headmen and bands of archers recruited from among their followers. He was present when a batch of about 200 prisoners were tried by Cleveland Saheb, with only hill chiefs as assessors, for having carried off 900 head of cattle from Kharakpur. After a three days' trial two chiefs were condemned to death, and hanged next morning from the tree under which the court had been held. Another was condemned to death and seven more to life-long confinement unless they delivered up the stolen cattle within 20 days. He remembered Keating Saheb, too, the first Collector of Birbhum, who had even more power over the Santals, wholly putting down their raiding by a hand that was at once strong and free, and inducing them to follow peaceful pursuits. Then the Government, having protected the Lowlanders from these wild Highlanders, also took measures to provide an asylum for the hillmen, where they could cultivate the land in peace. A ring of masonry pillars was erected in Birbhum, to mark out a reserve for the hillmen. The Santals soon monopolised the fertile valleys, leaving the barren hills to the Paharias and other less enterprising tribes.

Old Manka had had four sons, but all were dead except Budhu. The eldest had died of cholera, a few months after his marriage. The second, when a lad of sixteen, was herding goats in the jungle one day when a thunderstorm came on. He gathered his flock for shelter into one of the recesses of the trunk of a huge semal tree. It was struck by lightning, and both the herd and all the goats were killed. The third son was herding cows one day on the further side of the river. Heavy rain came on, the river was flooded, and when the time for taking the cows home came near, he tried to cross holding on to the tail of the biggest cow. He sank in mid-stream,—pulled down, the people said, by the demon or *bonga* of the river. The eldest son is always called the Big One *(maranič)*; the second son is the Little One *(hudinič)*, till num er three arrives. Then he is called the Middle One *(taluič)*, and Middle One he remains, how ever many more there may be. The third is the *sanjla*, the fourth the *manjhla* son. There were two daughters, but both had married, and gone to their husbands' homes in distant villages. Great, therefore, was the old man's joy when the birth of a son's son secured the male succession for another generation.

The first great event in the new friend's life was the naming, or *Narta*, a ceremony which takes place three, five, or seven days after the birth. Until it was over, both parents were ceremonially unclean, and no one would take food or drink in their house. Old Manka was determined to celebrate the birth in style, so the whole village was invited on the fifth day as well as relatives from a distance. The men, having shaved, went to the river to bathe. On their return an infusion of pounded neem leaves mixed with rice was offered as a libation to the household demon,—a god sacred to each house, whose name is a secret cherished by the father and whispered by him when dying into the ear of his eldest surviving son. This offering was made to secure for the new friend the god's protection and goodwill. The guests then sipped a little of the bitter mixture themselves. Then Budhu solemnly named the child Manka, after his own father, according to custom in the case of the firstborn when he is a boy. The *dhai* or midwife (she had received a fee of one rupee for presiding at the birth; it would have been eight annas had it been a girl) then went round the company sprinkling a little flour and water on the breast of each individual, and repeating the name as she did so.

The whole company was then regaled from huge earthen pots of rice beer, the brewing of which was one of the things the first parents of the human race taught their offspring. A feast followed. Several pigs were killed and chopped up entire, including bones and bristles. They were cooked as four separate dishes,—the flesh, the bones, the entrails, the juice,—and a supply of each was served out to every guest, with boiled rice and dal.

Little Manka's full name was Manka Murmu, Murmu being the name of the sept or sub-tribe to which he belonged by birth. There are twelve of these septs, seven of which are descended from the seven sons of Pilchu Haram and Pilchu Budhi, the Santal Adam and Eve. They are Hasdak, Murmu, Kisku, Hembron, Marndi, Soren and Tudu. Five more, Baske, Besra, Pauria, Chore, and Bedea, were subsequently added, having originated in different ways. Pauria and Chore, for example, mean Pigeon and Lizard, and these names were first applied as nicknames to some members of a big hunting party who succeeded in killing nothing but these harmless creatures. The number of sub-septs is almost indefinite. So among the Santals themselves he was Manka Murmu, but to the outside world Manka Manjhi. Among the Santals *manjhi*, strictly speaking, means the village headman or *tikadar*, but it is also used as a proper name. In the bazaar and in the cutcherry every Santal is called *manjhi* and if any one asks a Santal in Hindi or Bengali what his caste is, he replies *manjhi log*. If asked in Santali, he will say he is a *Hor*,—which means a Man, the name used by the Santals to designate themselves.

But the naming was not yet final. There was a strong prejudice against using the name too often, for the *bongas* would learn it, and their knowledge of it would give them more power for evil over the child. So another name was adopted—as usual a nickname—for common use. This name was Matla, or Drunken. Manka was the child's real, or, as the people put it, his *inner* name, Matla was his *upper* name, by which he was generally called, as a "blind" to the demons. He had as many terms of endearment applied to him, too, as heart could wish. He was his mother's *sona beta*, her golden boy; he was lord of the country and king of them all. And he had reproachful names, too. If he cried too much, his mother would say, "Now stop your crying, little one, or the people will say you are the son of a Hindu.." Then he also was the means of giving names to other people. Till he came, his father and mother had never addressed each other by name, and the former was known to the world as Budhu's bride. Now to each other and to every one else he was *Manka apat*, the father of Manka and she was *Manka engat*, the mother of Manka, and the household collectively were *Mankateko* which is the Santali way of saying Manka and Company.

Every day Manka was smeared all over with mustard-oil and put out in the sun to frizzle. His father made a hammock for him out of bark-rope, and slung it from the eaves of the house. As a young infant he was a *bale* (ba-le); when he was able to sit erect he was called, strange to say, a *sidup'*, and when he began to toddle he was a *caco* (pronounced chacho, *c* in Santali always having the sound of *ch* in 'church'). For a year he was fed entirely on his mother's milk. Then he got boiled rice as well, but continued to supplement it from the maternal breast till his little sister Maeno was born when he was three years old. (This is not physiological, but it is true.). Another child born in Taletandi about the same time had lost its mother from fever when he was three weeks old. The father had done his best. He tried to feed the child with a dirty rag dipped in dirty milk, and had extemporized a rude feeding bottle of bamboo with a rolled up leaf for a mouth-piece. Then he got a goat to suckle the child, but the little mite dwindled and died, as nearly all the young children did when derived of their mother's care.

Manka's only article of clothing in those days was a string tied round his waist, which served a useful as well as an ornamental purpose. It automatically warned him when he had eaten or drunk enough. A cowrie shell, one of the commonest amulets throughout the East, and a small brass bell were attached to the cord, and as long as the bell was heard to tinkle Manka's mother knew where to find him. But Manka and his mother were seldom separated. While working about the house she always had her eye upon him, and when she went to fetch water or firewood or to buy or sell at the market, she carried him astride the left hip. One day she had taken him into the jungle, and having spread a cloth under a shady tree, had laid him there while she went to search for firewood. Hearing a scream, she turned to see a tiger making off with her child in its jaws. Quick as thought, she sprang after him, and with a small hatchet which she had brought with her for lopping the dead branches off trees, with all her might she dealt the brute a blow between the eyes. With a roar it dropped its prey and bounded away. Next day it was found lying dead at a short distance with its skull fractured. Manka's mother carried him home and applied a poultice of neem leaves to his wounds. Thanks to his plumpness they were only flesh deep and they healed up, but to his dying day Manka carried the marks of the tiger's teeth on his shoulder. About the same time another child was carried off by a wolf, by far the most ferocious and daring of the beasts of prey, from a charpoy within the courtyard, in full daylight, before its mother's eyes. She raised a hue and cry, and the neighbours joined her in pursuit. When an arrow whizzed close to the wolf's head, it feared it was being overtaken, but, determined not to relinquish its spoil entirely, it put down the child and tore a mouthful from its side before it fled. The child lingered for a few days, but its wounds were beyond the range of domestic surgery and proved mortal.

Before Manka was three years old, he had done one very clever thing without knowing it: he had learned the Santali language. Had he known all the long-sounding names which grammarians afterwards gave to the twenty-five tenses of the Santali verb, his little head would have been turned; but he was quite unconscious of having done anything extraordinary. And the strange thing was that from the first he picked his way through the intricacies of the language without a mistake. An English child finds the pronouns a difficulty, but Manka had many more to grapple with, and conquered them all. There was a dual as well as a plural, and in both dual and plural there were two forms, the inclusive and the exclusive. Thus he had to learn to distinguish four different words for *us*—*aliñ* we two (you and I); *alañ* we two (I and some one else); *abo*, we (more than two, including the person addressed); *ale*, we (more than two, excluding the person addressed). Then all these and the other pronouns went into the verb, which contained within itself both subject and object, and possessive and dative as well. Thus, "The boy struck me" was *Koras dalkediña*—*dal* being the root of the verb 'to strike.' But if two boys struck Manka, he had to say *Korakin dalkediñakin*, and if there were more than two aggressors *Korako dalkediñako*. Here the object *me* was the same throughout. If Manka said 'I struck the dog' it was *Seta iñ dalkedeañ*. If he said *dalketkinañ* it meant there were two dogs struck, and if *dalketkoañ* that there were more than two. If he said "I struck his dog," the possessive 'his' had also to go into the verb—*Seta iñ dalkedataeañ*—being represented by *tae*. If he said to his mother "I am working for you" the dative had to go into the verb likewise,—*Iñ kamiamkanañ*—the *am* in the middle of the verb meaning 'for you.' Then he had also to distinguish many fine shades of meaning in the tenses of the verb. "Has your father come home?" his mother would ask him. If he used the perfect in reply, *Hečakanae*, it would be understood to mean strictly that the father had just come. If he used one of the past tenses, *Hečenae*, it would mean that the father had come and was then there. If he used another past tense, *Hečlenae* it would mean that he had come but gone away again. It was a comfort, however, that the language was remarkably uniform, with few dialectical differences, and being entirely a spoken language there was no distinction between the colloquial and the literary. So once Manka had mastered the *hor ror*, as it was called, it carried him throughout the length and breadth of the Santal country. In the matter of moral as well as of literary education, Manka was left largely to the light of nature. When he was in a violent temper, he hammered his mother, and she, poor woman, never thought of retaliating. Of his father he had a more wholesome dread, but a scolding was the most severe punishment he ever received. A Santal might occasionally chastise his wife, his child almost never. When Manka was just in a huff, he sat at the back of the house, where the "midden" was located. This was a sort of passive resistance, or the equivalent of being on strike. If his mother wisely let him alone, hunger soon drove him back to respectability and conventionality. He was taught, more by example than by precept, to speak the truth, and to fear nothing that was of the earth earthy. But from earliest years his little world was peopled with malignant demons ever on the watch to do him harm.

CHAPTER III.

MANKA'S BOYHOOD.

MANKA'S childhood may be said to have ended and his boyhood to have begun when his father, by means of a burning rag, branded him with three marks on the outer aspect of his left forearm, above the wrist. These marks, called *sikha*, are to be found on every male Santal. Manka was six years old at this time and had a little brother now, whose inner name was Chatur, the Clever One, but who was soon more generally known by his upper name, Chede or Bald head.

Although Manka, in common with other Santal children, began very early to take his share in the work of the farm,—holding the plough, harrowing, sowing, reaping, threshing, felling timber, herding cattle, milking the cows,—it was by no means a case of all work and no play. The first duty entrusted to him was that of herding the cattle. All the village boys clubbed together, drove their combined herds to the jungle in the morning, brought them back to the shelter of their sheds for two hours at midday, drove them out in the afternoon, and brought them home in the evening. As in Isaiah's time, each ox knew its owner, and every cow its master's crib. They were all driven in a mass up the village street, and each beast turned into the right courtyard when it came to it. If it did not, it and all its female relatives became the objects of boundless vituperation. Sheep and goats were herded along with the cows, but the buffaloes kept hours and rules of their own. In spite of their bulk, they were regarded as delicate creatures, unable to bear the heat and burden of the day. They were kept inside for a much longer siesta, and were kept out two hours longer in the evening. In the hot weather they were herded by night, and were hardly to be trusted in a cart, lest they should make a bolt for any tank or river that came within view. They were never happier than when their herds made them lie down in a shady pool in the river and threw water over their backs or slabbered them with mud. They were lazy stupid-looking monsters, but there were stories current among the boys of buffaloes who had defended their herd laddies from the attacks of tigers, forming a ring round them and repelling the assaults successfully with their horns.

The herds, boys and girls, had words of command which the cattle all understood, and to which they readily responded. To the cows they called *ihiť ihiť* to summon them, and *hijaǩ hijaǩ* to drive them away. To the buffaloes the cry was *dur heť dur heť* to make them come, and *harjaǩ harjaǩ* to make them go. There were common calls for the sheep and goats—*dorae dorae* to summon them, *hedok hedok* to drive them. *Dur dur* was the pigs' call. *Leh leh* summoned a dog to heel, *liliao* hounded it on. *Curu curu* was the call for peafowl, *ti ti ti ti* for ordinary fowls, and *tai tai* for domesticated pigeons. There were two things every herd boy carried with him to the jungle to beguile the time. One was the flute, which they all knew how to make as well as to play, although some were better at it than others. It was made by cutting a hollow bamboo just below two successive joints, so that one end was open, the other closed, and burning the holes with a redhot iron. Flute-playing, like brewing rice beer, was an art inherited from the first parents of the race, and wherever there were Santals the jungle resounded with the

> "Notes, with many a winding bout
> Of linkèd sweetness long drawn out."

The other part of each herd boy's equipment consisted of his bow and arrows. Manka had begun to make toy bows and arrows as soon as he could toddle about by himself. When six years old he killed his first bird, and two years later he proudly brought home a hare for the family pot when he brought the cattle in at night. The bow was of bamboo of sufficient length to reach up to the lobe of the owner's ear when placed upright on the ground. The "strings" used were of two kinds, one a real string of fibre, the other a thin strip of bamboo. The arrows were of various patterns, distinguished chiefly as sharp or blunt. The blunt arrow-heads, made of bamboo, horn, iron, or the fruit of the *lopong* tree (*Terminalia belerica*), were used for killing birds and other small game, and also for knocking the fruit from the high branches of trees. The sharp arrowheads, of iron, were flat or round. The shafts, made of bamboo or the culms of various tall grasses, were feathered at the ends. A fibre string was pulled by the thumb and index finger, but the boys could do more deadly execution with the bamboo string, which they pulled, not with thumb and index finger, but by grasping it firmly with the index and middle fingers. One day when all the men and boys of Taletandi, having left the cattle to the care of their wives and sisters, were acting as beaters for the Collector of Birbhum, who was in camp in their neighbourhood, a Rajput peon noticed the boys using their bows and arrows in this way. "That is just like the Bhils in my country," he said, "Long ago a Raja caught them hunting without permission in his preserves, and to prevent them from doing it again he had all their thumbs cut off. But they soon learned to pull the bowstring with their fingers." The boys sometimes tied two strings to a bow, joined them by a little string network at the middle part, and propelled stones in this way as if from a sling. Pigeons they often caught alive by means of a snare and a decoy bird, the lids of whose eyes they pinned together with thorns to make it sit still, or by means of a birdlime prepared from the juice of the banyan tree. Quails and partridges, too, they kept as pets, carrying them about with them in cages made of sticks and leaves, and they taught them to sing while they whistled an accompaniment. In the rainy season they fished in the rice-fields, either with hook and line or by setting traps at the broken places in the embankments where the surplus water rushed from a higher to a lower field. The fish they caught in this way were often of a good size, as they had found their way up into the fields from the rivers.

The boys were all born naturalists and knew every tree and shrub, every fruit and flower, in the jungle, and they also seemed to enjoy the confidence of all the birds and beasts and creeping things. Anyone who got hold of a new fact in natural history was very proud of his find. "How does the jackal get rid of fleas"? Manka asked his companions one day. "Who knows?" was the general reply—for a Santal never says he does not know; he covers his own lack of knowledge under an insinuation of universal ignorance. "Well, I'll tell you. He balances a little bit of stick or a leaf on the tip of his snout, and walks slowly into a tank. As he gets deeper and deeper the fleas climb higher and higher, until they are all on his head. Then he slowly sinks his head, until they take refuge on the stick or leaf. Then he ducks his nose under water and they all float away."

They had their superstitions, too. A bigger boy once saw Manka killing a frog by beating its head with a stone. "Don't do that," he said, "or your ear will suppurate." "Are you sure of that?" another boy asked. "My little brother's ear suppurated last year, but we thought it was a lizard he had killed." If a boy was stung by a wild bee—which occasionally happened when a nest was being raided for honey—he if possible caught the bee, pulled out its entrails and applied them to the wound. That was regarded as an infallible cure.

Propounding riddles and telling stories were also favourite amusements with the boys as they tended their cows in the jungle or sat round the fire in the threshing-floor at night during the harvest season, watching the rice and other grains. Riddles were often played as a regular game, the boys taking sides and firing their conundrums at each other. If the side attacked failed to guess aright, they were hailed with derisive cries, such as "What jungly country do you come from?" and others in the style of "Does your mother know you're out?" These riddles betrayed a humorous turn of mind, and often a very fertile imagination as well as habits of observation. The word for a riddle is *Kudum*, aud the proposition of a riddle was always preceded by the formula *Kudum kurit kurit* which had just as much meaning as fee-fo-fum. One riddle was "O five brothers, carry me beyond the white stones." This was supposed to be spoken by food to the five fingers, the white stones being the teeth. Another was: "Who is the man who carries about with him everywhere a crooked stick?" Answer: a dog and its tail. Another was: "Who is the old woman who can run down a hill but cannot climb up again?" Answer: water. Another was: "Two sisters sitting on one stool, but never touching each other." Answer: any animal's horns. Another was: "A child who says in the mornings, 'Come, let us eat flesh'." Answer: The goad used for driving buffaloes. "A fair girl carrying a black pot" was the *bhelwa* fruit, the black nut being surrounded at its base by a yellow pericarp. "A crooked thing that makes other things straight" was the adze. "He who rides upon a buffalo in the hot season and upon a pig in the cold season" was the sun, the Santal pig, consisting of little except skin and bone, being regarded as one of the swiftest of four-footed things.

Then they would often try to cap each other's stories. One boy would tell how the moon one day said to the sun, "You eat up your children (the day stars) and then I shall eat up mine." So the sun ate her children, the day stars, and the moon wickedly refused to follow suit. So the sun has ever since been chasing the moon but has never been able to catch it. Another boy would add that that reminded him of a story he once heard from a man who came from the hills in the far north. The sun one day became mortally offended because the beasts in the forest had laughed at him. So he hid himself behind a high hill and refused to shine. The beasts were greatly distressed and sent several deputations to him to plead for forgiveness and a restitution of former favours. At last the sun said he was willing to shine again on one condition—the beasts must appoint some one to waken him in good time every morning. To this the beasts agreed, and entrusted this duty to the cock.

But the old men were the best storytellers, and Manka often got his grand-father to tell him one of his many tales as they sat together in the threshing-floor. The stories were of the orthodox kind about poor boys who married kings' daughters, and cruel step-mothers and magic lamps and wonder-working spirits and talking animals—such stories as are found everywhere, in one form or another, east and west. Here is one of old Manka's stories, a very familar one, in the form in which it was current among the Santals: "There was once a girl who had six brothers who were all married. They were all merchants and were often away from home for many days at a time. On these occasions their wives for some reason or other took every means of vexing and worrying their sister-in-law, whom they hated. One time they ordered her to go out to the jungle to bring a bundle of firewood without tying it together. But a big rock snake took pity upon her in her distress and tied himself round the bundle, only stipulating that she should put it down gently when she reached home. This made the sisters-in-law still more angry, and they told her to go and bring the milk of a tigress, in a small earthen vessel they gave her. On reaching the tiger's den she found only two cubs there, who on hearing her story concealed her in the den, and on their mother's return managed to secure a little of her milk in the vessel and to enable the girl to get away with it in safety. The sisters-in-law again tried to get rid of her by sending her to bring bear's milk, but the bear's cubs befriended her in the same way. Then they told her to bring water from the spring in a water pot that had a hole in it. This time a frog came to the rescue, and by sitting on the hole kept the water from running out. The sisters-in-law then poured out a basketful of mustard-seed on the ground, and ordered her to gather it all up. A flock of pigeons had compassion on her and picked up all the seed. Then she was sent to gather leaves for making plates, with nothing to tie them. The little grass snake helped her this time, tying himself into a knot round the bundle. The sisters-in-law at last told her to climb up a high tree to bring down some flowers from the highest branch, with which they would deck their hair on the occasion of her marriage. When she had ascended the tree, they tied thorny bushes round the trunk to prevent her from coming down, and left her there. It so happened that her brothers on their way home rested for a little under this tree. A tear-drop from their sister's eye fell on the hand of one of them, and looking up he recognised her high up among the branches. They quickly brought her down, and she told them everything. They were indignant, and putting their sister into a sack carried her home on a bullock's back. When their wives came out to welcome them, the brothers asked "Where is our sister?" but got no reply. Afterwards the brothers dug a deep well and on the pretence of propitiating the water demon induced their wives to stand round the well mouth with offerings in their hands. At a given signal each man hurled his wife down the well, and they then placed a cart over the opening. Their sister after that used to go to the well, and looking down she would say—'You treated me cruelly once, but boo, sisters, boo.'

CHAPTER IV.

MANKA'S BOYHOOD.—*(Continued)*:

OFTEN the stories old Manka told professed to be authentic history of no very remote period, and he told them boldly, troubled by no fear of destructive criticism. One day little Manka accompanied the old man to Deoghar. There was neither salt nor tobacco in the house—food was insipid without the one and life itself without the other,—and he was taking a few tasar cocoons to exchange for these commodities. It happened to be February and the festival which is supposed to celebrate the marriage of Mahadeo to Parbati was being celebrated. Nineteen of the Deoghur temples are dedicated to Mahadeo, and three to his wife. The pinnacles of the former were united by silken ropes, some of them forty yards long—to the pinnacles of the latter, and from these ropes were suspended gaily-coloured cloths, garlands of flowers, and tawdry tinsel ornaments. Pilgrims were there in thousands from all parts of India, and their shouts made an incessant din. Crowds were everywhere, and old Manka with difficulty elbowed his way through to the bazaar, where he pointed out to his grandson three huge stones, two upright and one horizontal, each twelve feet long and said to be seven tons in weight, which stood at the entrance to the main street, and which were said to have been objects of worship among the jungle tribes of an earlier day. Having executed their business and got clear of the crowd, the two Mankas started on their long tramp homewards. "Mahadeo and Parbati!" the old man said, after a long silence, "they little know that the place is named after one of *our* ancestors, my boy." He then told the following story: "Many many years ago, long before the temples were built, some Brahmins came to settle beside the lake at Deoghur. They erected the emblem of Mahadeo and for some time they worshipped it faithfully. The jungle people around still came to the place to worship the three stones. But the land was good, and the Brahmins became rich and lazy. They gave themselves up to a bad life and neglected their god. Some of the jungle people were shocked by the evil deeds of the Brahmins, and one of them, Baiju by name, made a vow that to show the contempt in which he held them he would beat their god with a club every day before he touched food. This he did regularly, and the Brahmins cared nothing. But one morning Baiju's cows strayed into the forest and were lost. He sought them all day and came home late at night, hungry and weary. He was sitting down to his food when he suddenly remembered his vow, and tired as he was he went off at once and gave Mahadeo his customary drubbing. Then all at once a most beautiful form, sparkling with jewels, rose up from the middle of the lake and addressed him thus: 'Behold, the man forgets hunger and weariness to beat me, while my own priests give themselves up to lust and neglect to give me either food or drink. Let him ask me what he will, and I shall give it to him.' Baiju answered: 'I am strong and rich, the leader of my people, and with cattle in abundance. What more do I want? You are called Lord (*Nath*). Let me too be called Lord, and let this temple of yours be known by my name.' 'Granted,' said the deity; 'from to-day you are Baijunath and my temple here shall be known by your name.' Now all over India this shrine is known among the Hindus by the name of Baijnath."

At other times old Manka told how the world was created at the beginning out of a great watery waste. The Great Spirit, *Marang Buru*, with the help of a tortoise, (a crab and the earth-worm king having failed), raised the earth, and seeds of grass were sown to make it firm. Then the first human pair, Pilchu Haram and Pilchu Budhi, were born from two eggs laid by a wild goose. The Great Spirit clothed them, five yards of cloth for the man, six for the woman, and showed them how to brew rice beer from the yeast he gave them. Seven sons and seven daughters were born, and so the race was established. But afterwards, when a deluge of rain-fire destroyed the inhabitants of the earth, a single pair were preserved in the cleft of a mountain. After that, as the race multiplied, the Great Spirit became jealous of them, for they all spoke the same language and lived together in peace and happiness. So he contrived a plan to sow dissension among them, that he might rule over them more easily. He summoned the people to run a race for prizes he had prepared. These prizes were five in number, consisting of various kinds of food placed in leaf cups of different sizes. In the first was beef, in the second goat's flesh, in the third fish, in the fourth plantains, in the fifth rice and milk. The man who came in first naturally chose the beef, of which there was a larger quantity than of any other kind of food, and he became the father of the Santal race. The second man chose the goat's flesh and founded the Mahomedan community. The man who got the fish was the originator of one caste of Hindus, while he who took the plantains was the first Chatri. The last to arrive had to be content with rice and milk and he became the progenitor of the Brahmins.

But the Santals, old Manka added, were not always known as Santals. They were once Kherwars, a powerful and wealthy people, owning the land they cultivated, with kings and armies of their own. Nor in those days were they demon-worshippers. When they lived in the land of Chai, where they built a stronghold called Champa, their kings were of the Kisku sept. One of these kings took secretly as his concubine a girl from the Birhor tribe—a tribe of wandering gipsies who make a living mainly by hunting and rope-making. A son was born of this alliance, named Madho Sing. He was born in the jungle where his mother and other women were gathering bamboo shoots for food. The other women asked the mother, "Which are you going to take home, the bamboos or the child?" She replied, "I shall have many more children, but who knows if I shall find more bamboos?" So she covered the child with leaves and left him. That evening the King's four daughters, with their girl friends, were walking in the jungle, and hearing the child's cries they found him, carried him home, and adopted him. When Madho Sing grew up, he became the King's Dewan, collected all his rents, and carried a golden umbrella. One day he said to the King, "Get me a wife, or I shall marry one of your daughters by force." So the King asked his people to provide a wife for Madho Sing, but they all refused, saying that no one knew who his father was or to what tribe he belonged. Then Madho Sing said he would marry whom he pleased by force and the people said to the King, "Come, let us flee, or he will defile us all." Those who fled became the Santals. First, by the King's advice, they made carts to convey their goods, all the carts being of exactly the same size and pattern, so that they could go in a line and leave a track, as of only one cart. Starting off one night by stealth, they soon came to a flooded river which they could not cross. Then they began to pray to all the objects around them, stocks and stones, trees and shrubs, promising to worship any of them if they would help them across. Nag and Nagin, a serpent and his mate, responded, and kept back the river with their bodies until all were across. They came to a door of stone, which they could not open. They were almost in despair when two of their number said, "Call upon the *bongas* (demons), while we break through the door with the ends of our bows." In this way they passed through and a second door that stood in their way was opened in the same manner. In the morning, Madho Sing, finding they had fled, girded on his sword, seized his battle-axe, and followed in pursuit. All along the way he came across traces of their demon worship, the stones here and there being smeared with red paint. He overtook them at the Partridge Rock in the land of Sant, where they had settled down. They had been told that when they reached this place each household should kill a bullock, eat its flesh, and spread the hide on the top of their leaf hut. When Madho Sing saw these evidences of demon worship and of cow-killing his scorn and disgust knew no bounds: "You are no more Kherwars," he said to them; "your caste is gone—you are vile cow-eaters. From now you will be known as Santals." He then left them and returned home. So ended the Santals' golden age, for the return of which they have ever since been longing in vain. Since then they have worshipped the *bongas* and eaten all kinds of flesh, including that of animals that have died by accident or disease. They have had many wanderings, and wherever they have gone they have danced the ground hollow, drank the water springs dry, and worn the grass off the face of the earth.

Occasionally, the boys played games, chiefly in the moonlight evenings during the hot weather. These games, like the stories, bore a strong resemblance to those in vogue among children elsewhere. One was called *Hedelguda.* The players were ranged on two sides of a line drawn on the ground. One boy from one side would dart across the line to the other side, uttering the following rigmarole without drawing breath—*Hedelgud huwan huwa banga bairi cura raja bher partapur kher partapur kher.* If he drew breath, he could be caught, and was then "dead." If, without drawing breath, he caught others, they were "dead." When a boy became "dead," another boy, "the avenger of blood," from his side could come across the line repeating the formula without drawing breath. If *he* was caught while saying the words, and before he had drawn breath, he was dead; if he was not caught his pursuers were dead and the dead man of his own side was alive again. When only one boy was left alive on either side he was a "dummy," (*gunga*). He refused to speak, laugh, or smile, or make any sound, and until the boys of the other side could force some sound from him by tickling him, squeezing him, or sitting upon him, the game was not won. When one side had won the game, sides were changed and the game was played over again as before. Another popular game was called Peafowl's Egg; why, nobody could tell. All the boys except one sat down in a circle, facing the centre. This one, Manka, for instance, twisted a piece of cloth very tightly like a rope. When it was ready, he commanded all the boys to bend their heads so as not to see him, and began running round outside the circle. He dropped the twisted cloth behind one of the boys but continued to run round. If the boy behind whose back the cloth was dropped was aware that it was there, he jumped up and began running round with the cloth and Manka sat down in his place. If he was not aware of it, when Manka reached him on the next round he took up the cloth and struck him with it with all his might. Manka then ran on to repeat the trick on some one else.

Another game was to stand round a circle drawn on the ground. The leader repeated a formula of nonsensical phrases, and immediately on its conclusion all the boys gave a jump. The boy who was last to jump became the *hadi* and had to stand within the ring. The others then danced round the ring shouting, and the *hadi* had to try to scratch them. When he succeeded in scratching a boy, that boy had to join him within the circle. When the number of boys within the circle was equal to that of the boys still outside, the game resolved itself into a contest between those within and those without, the boys outside trying to pull the inside boys out; the insides trying to pull the outsiders in. The last boy left outside or inside became the *hadi* for a fresh round of the game. Another boisterous game was to blindfold a boy, put a stick in his hand, and tell him to smash an old earthen pot that he had seen lying a few feet in front of him. When he advanced cautiously, raised his stick and then brought it down with great force on the ground, probably a foot or two wide of the pot, there was a roar of laughter from the onlookers. Another amusement was dancing. There were the stated festivals when they danced for days and nights on end, and they were always willing to take part in the celebrations of the Durga Puja and other Hindu festivals in the same way. But there were less formal dances, held at any place or time, as they felt inclined. There were special dances for special festivals and for marriages;

there was a dance that was danced by the men alone when camping out during the annual hunt, and there was the sword and shield dance; but there were other dances that could be danced on all occasions. The sexes did not dance together—that would have been considered the height of impropriety. The women or girls, sometimes with their hair decked with living fireflies, formed a line shoulder to shoulder, in the form of an arc of a circle. Singing, and in some cases beating their cymbals, they advanced towards the centre and retreated again, with a peculiar wavy movement, and at the same time moving very slowly to the right. Within this area the boys disported themselves, some playing their flutes, others beating their drums, and all of them leaping and capering and making fools of themselves generally. It is difficult to follow the meaning of the songs, which the girls sang over and over again, as they were full of allegory and parable, but the following is a free translation of one of them:—

"Come, Maku, come, and stand among us all.
No, I cannot come, I hear my mother call.
The milk flower is my mother;
She would be scolding me.
The king flower is my brother;
He would be beating me.
My father in the forest stands,
All decked and gay with flowery bands.
They all say that I must not go,
And so my answer must be, No."

Heard from a distance the combination of female voices, flutes, drums, and cymbals made a pleasant harmony One of the officials in every Santal village is the *jog manjhi*, an important functionary at marriages and at the ceremonies that precede them and also in a general way the custodian of the morals of the young people. Any breach of decorum at a dance was reported to him and he took measures to put things right. As a rule he was present at the dances himself.

Manka's boyhood may be said to have come to an end with a ceremony known as the *Chatiar*. There was no fixed time for it, but it was supposed to mark the formal admission of the lad into Santal Society, with the recognition of all his rights and privileges as a member thereof. Until it was performed he could not marry, and if he died without its having been performed, he was denied the honour dear to the Santal's heart, of having a fragment of his bones carried to the Damudar River. In Manka's case the ceremony took place when he was about fifteen years old (for nobody now remembered how old he was, although his mother could always tell that it was a few weeks before the rice harvest when he was born). The grandfather had a liberal supply of rice beer brewed, and invited all the villagers and relatives to partake of it. "This is the grandfather's beer," he said to them while serving them, and when the ceremony was completed he stood up before the assembly and said: "We appeal to you five men (a figurative phrase); we were black like crows, now we are white as the white paddy bird; you five men are our witnesses."

Manka's friends were now free to begin the negotiations in connection with what they considered the most important event in his life—his marriage. But that must form the subject of another chapter.

CHAPTER V.

COURTSHIP AND MARRIAGE.

FROM the day of Manka's birth his marriage was a thing taken for granted. It never occurred to his parents or other friends that it was a matter about which he himself should be consulted. He was not, it is true, married in infancy to another infant, but it is true that he did not see his bride till the wedding day. His marriage was a great occasion, for which elaborate preparations had to be made, and which was celebrated regardless of expense, with a royal profusion of eating and drinking, dancing and singing.

Among the Santals there are marriages which are carried through without much ceremony, as when a man takes a second wife, his first being still alive, or when a widower marries a widow. There are marriages, too, *in formâ pauperis*, as when a bride, instead of being wedded in her father's house, goes to the bridegroom's house and so saves a great deal of expenditure. Another way to do it on the cheap is to give a daughter in exchange for a son-in-law, or *vice versâ*. Or a poor lad who cannot afford to do the thing in style can enter the matrimonial state as a *ghardi jawae*, going to live with his father-in-law, and working for him in payment for the bride. Probably in the latter case there is some defect or blemish on the girl's part to reconcile the parents to disposing of her in this undignified way. Then there are marriages which, although irregular, are not illegal. One of these is called "buying a husband," as distinguished from the "bride buying" as the orthodox marriage is designated. A girl may have been wronged by a man who ought to marry her, but is prevented from doing so by reason of his sept or relationship. He must then settle on the girl a sufficient endowment to induce some one else to marry her. Then a girl who has set her heart upon a man, can, if she cares to do so, practically force herself upon him by entering his house and spending a night there. This is called the "running in" marriage A young Lochinvar, on the other hand, can make the girl of his choice his own in spite of her relatives by taking her unawares and marking her forehead with red paint. Or a young couple may simply elope The Santals show an extreme reluctance to fasten upon any children the stigma of illegitimacy, if it can possibly be avoided, and all these forms of marriage, however much they may be disapproved of, are regarded as legal. A married man may even take another woman into his family as a temporary second wife until her child is born, in order that this child may be publicly recognised as his son or daughter. Then mother and child may go their way with the present of a cow.

Manka made an honourable and conventional marriage, the observances connected with which it will take some time to describe and a good deal of patience to follow.

The first law of marriage among the Santals is that a man must not marry within his own, that is, his father's sept. He may take a wife from his mother's sept if she is not within the forbidden limits of consanguinity or affinity, which among the Santals extend to a very remote degree. This law is as inviolable as any ever promulgated by Mede or Persian. There is a Scottish proverb that it is better to wed "over the midden than over the moor," but the Santals incline to the opposite belief. A bride is very seldom chosen from the bridegroom's village. She is sought for somewhere on the other side of the hill.

When Manka was about sixteen years old, the first step was taken by choosing a go-between or groomsman, a middle-aged married man named Bhola. He was commissioned in the first place to seek a bride, and the world was all before him, where to choose,—within the confines of the Santal tribe, of course, and outside the limits already described. Taletandi was one of a small group of isolated Santal villages. The bulk of the Santal population in that part of the country at that time was in the Daman-i-Koh ("Skirts of the hill"), to which there had been a steady immigration from the Singbhum direction since 1836. It was to the village of Baromasia in this region that Bhola was led to direct his steps. His first approaches were circuitous. "Have you any pearls to sell?" he asked the head of a certain house. "That depends upon the quality of your diamonds," was the reply. The result was that Bhola reported to Manka's father that he thought he knew where a suitable mate for his son was to be found. Thereupon Manka's father and grandfather and a few relatives set out to inspect the bride and her surroundings. While engaged on this expedition they attached the utmost importance to omens they might encounter on the way. So they set off with the first streak of light, without seeing or being seen by the other villagers, and Bhola went before them as they approached Baromasia to warn unpropitious portents out of their way. If they saw anyone either carrying firewood or chopping it, or even a man with an axe over his shoulder; or a woman washing clothes, throwing away ashes, or lighting a fire; if a jackal crossed their path or they raised a quail or hare; or if it rained,—these were bad omens. But it was a good omen if the first sight that met them on arriving at the bride's village was a cow or a corpse or a woman carrying a water-pot on her head, or if they heard the cry of a certain bird on the right hand or of another bird on the left.

Manka's friends were fortunate in avoiding all the bad omens, so they were not discouraged by the fact that it was so dark when they reached Baromasia that they were not able to discern anything very clearly that could be interpreted as a good omen. The object of their visit was no secret, Bhola having prepared the way, and soon after their arrival at the house two young women, with a girl of about fourteen between them, advanced towards them, and Bhola said to Manka's father, "It is the middle one, take a good look at her." So Maku enters our story.

Maku was the eldest daughter of Thakra, of the Tudu sept. She was born in the Daman-i-Koh, where her father was one of the early settlers from the south-west. The Santals did not then enjoy all the privileges which had been granted to the other hillmen in this reserve, but they excelled them all in the rapidity with which they turned the jungle into fruitful fields. Maku received her grandmother's name as Manka had received his grandfather's. She was not branded on the arm as the boy had been but she was tattooed on the breast and arms by people of a tribe called Khudnis who made their living by doing this. The tattooing, however, was left incomplete till after her marriage. Then her husband would have it finished off at his own expense and so establish a claim to his wife which would be recognised in the world to come. A girl who died untattooed would fall a prey to huge serpents, thick as tree trunks, and boys who died unbranded would be food for worms of like dimensions.

At a very tender age Maku had learned to husk the rice in the early morning, to sweep out the house and courtyard and smear them with cow-dung, then to balance on her head an earthen pot almost as big as herself and fetch water from the spring, make plates and cups of *sal* leaves, to wash clothes with ashes for soap, and to cook rice and *dal*. She took her share in the field-work, too, uprooting and transplanting the seedlings of rice, hoeing the Indian corn, and reaping the various crops in harvest time. She knew all the edible roots and herbs in the jungle, where she went periodically with her mother to gather firewood, tooth-brushes, and leaves. At a later age she learned to spin the cotton she had helped to grow.

Manka's friends, having expressed their approval of Maku, offered five rupees as the price or *pon*, and this was accepted. *Dam* was never used to describe this transaction; *pon*, the term always employed, designated the purchase of tenant right, not of absolute possession. The next step was for Manka's friends to visit Manka's home to invest him with a *dhuti* or loin cloth. "Let us go and eat parched rice" was the wording of the invitation to this ceremony issued by Maku's father, and a party, about forty in number, set out under the guidance of Bhalu, who had arranged a suitable date with Manka's father. They were received with all the customary courtesies, including feet washing, and elaborate inquiries in stereotyped phrases were made regarding their health, in soul and body, flesh and skin. To these the spokesman of the visitors' party replied: "As you have been so good as to inquire, we tell you that, by your help and blessing, our spirits have expanded like a mountain, our bosoms have broadened out like bamboo mats, our beards have grown like horn trumpets." The time was spent in the exchange of compliments like this till the rice was cooked. Then the visitors stood in a ring round the courtyard where straw had been spread, till the headman of Taletandi gave the word of command, "Set your grain baskets on the ground," and all sat down together. Rice and *dal* were then served on leaf plates. During the meal nearly everything was referred to in veiled language. "Bring the frogs' platform, the peacocks are crying" meant, "Bring water, the guests are thirsty." "Shop-keepers' butter" was salt and "farmers' butter" was pepper.

So ended the day. In the morning the visitors were supplied with oil and tooth-brushes (twigs of trees) and shown where to bathe. Then light refreshments in the shape of parched rice and beer were served, and the parties having assembled in the courtyard the formal proceedings began. Manka, carrying a *lota* of water in his hand, was led out by his maternal uncle, who went round the guests, beginning with the headman of Taletandi, showing Manka what form of salutation was appropriate for each of them. Among the Santals, the *johar* is the equivalent of the *salaam* or *namuskar*, and it varies with almost every relationship. Manka followed his uncle, placing the *lota* of water before each person, and saluting in the proper way. Then he handed to each in turn a bowl of rice beer, which they all drank. Maku's father then grasped Manka with both hands and seated him on his own thigh. He then wound the *dhuti* round his waist and a *chadar* turban-wise round his head, and kissed him, to the accompaniment of an outburst of song by the women. Manka then served out another round of beer, in the strict order of precedence, and arrangements for a feast followed. The *jogmanjhi* of Taletandi placed an axe and a *lota* of water on a leaf plate before Maku's father, saying, "Come, Father Thakra, the tops of the pot-herbs are overripe, cut them down for us"—in other words, kill a goat. Then one of the house party held a goat, while one of the visitors killed it with the axe. The man who had held it tied some straw to the end of a stick and dipped it in the blood. The village priest of Taletandi then smeared cow-dung over the place where the goat had been slain and offered a libation of rice beer to the Sun god, the Great Spirit, and the deceased village chiefs. The slayer and the holder of the goat sat by his side, east and west. After offering the libation, he drank part of it. What remained was poured into two leaf cups and handed to him again. Crossing hands, he gave the cup in his left hand to the man on his right, and the cup in his right hand to the man on his left. Together they received it and together they drank it. If necessary this was repeated till the libation was consumed. The goat-holder with his blood-stained broom, followed by the slayer, then went round the company saluting, and Manka's father and Maku's father saluted each other in the form appropriate to their now established relationship as prospective parents-in law. After a few preliminaries, they grasped each other by the shoulders, drew their right shoulders together till they touched, and then the left, finishing up by giving each other a good shaking. Led by the groomsman, Maku's father went the round of Manka's friends, *joharing* each in the prescribed form. All the visitors then sat down, and after the exchange of a few more parables, the hosts cried, "The heads of the rice crop are ripe, down with your stumpy sickles," and all began to eat. The boiled rice and *dal*, and four dishes of goat-flesh, bones, entrails and juice, were served out three times. When a guest remarked, "Have the goats here no stomachs?" it was a hint that he had not received a helping of the second last dish, and the mistake was at once rectified. The guests having been abundantly satisfied, the hosts who had been serving them dined. Then once again forming into line the relatives saluted each other, and Maku's friends started off on their homeward journey with a supply of parched rice to eat by the way as a parting gift. So ended the Donning of the *Dhuti*.

Some months later it was followed by a ceremony called the Presentation of the Money *(Taka Chal)*, or the Binding Down of the Thatch. Maku's friends were then visited by Manka's, who by paying down an instalment of the *pon* and giving presents to the bride, clinched the bargain and made the betrothal complete. Arrangements having been made by the groomsman, the party set out, with a ram's horn and a drum, but without Manka himself. On arriving at Maku's village, they halted at the end of the street while Bhola went forward to announce their visit. Maku's father then summoned the headman of the village, his assistant or *paranik*, and the *jogmanjhi*, and his friends, and with drums they set out to meet the visitors, led by the *jogmanjhi* who carried a *lota* of water on a leaf plate. The parties met and saluted each other to music of the drums, and the visitors were conducted to a lodging place that had been prepared for them on the threshing floor, where they were supplied with cooking vessels, firewood, and leaf-plates for the food they had brought with them.

In the morning Manka's friends were summoned to Maku's house, whither they went with music, to be received and entertained with the same ceremonial courtesies that they had extended to Maku's friends at Taletandi. Then Manka's father handed a *sari* to the groomsman, who, entering the house, gave it to Maku's mother, who first handed it to Maku and then clothed her in it. Maku was then led out by her aunt who put a *lota* of water before each of the company in turn, Maku following and saluting, while her uncle served beer. When they reached Manka's father, he seated Maku on his thigh, placed a brass ornament round her neck, and kissed her. She, regaining her feet, bowed to him, and then presented first to him and then to the other guests a small bowl of beer. A few more of Manka's relatives also kissed her. Manka's father then gave two rupees to the groomsman, who, holding them in his fist, went round the company saluting and repeating the words, "We bind down the thatch." He then gave them to Maku's father who tested them, according to etiquette, not by the usual method of tossing them with the thumb nail, but by ringing them on the ground. Then the goat was killed as at the donning of the *dhuti*, the priest offered a libation of beer to the spirits in the same way, and a feast followed. "Have we filled the panniers?" the hosts asked. Those who had not yet eaten to satisfaction replied, "Your bullock, father, is not strong." Those who had finished said, "Our bullock is very strong." The feasting of the guests being finished, the *jogmanjhi* called to the attendant village maidens, "Come daughters, gather up the leaf-plates smartly. Now is the time they are watching you. If they are pleased with you, perhaps they will take you away too." The girls cleared away the soiled plates and cups, and Maku's friends then sat down to their own meal. When all had fed, Maku's friends once more ranged themselves round the courtyard and Manka's friends, led by the groomsman, went the round giving a final salutation before setting out on their return journey.

In the interval between this ceremony and the marriage proper, Manka's father sent a further instalment of two rupees to Maku's father by the hand of Bhola the groomsman. This was modestly called "Oil and Salt."

CHAPTER VI.

COURTSHIP AND MARRIAGE—*Continued.*

THESE ceremonies had taken place between the beginning of the year and the beginning of the rains The month of February in the following year was chosen for the final celebration of the marriage. The harvest work was over, and the preparation for the sowing of another crop had not yet begun. First Manka's father sent Bhola to Maku's father saying, "Shall we have the marriage this year? If so, shall we have it now before the leaves in the sacred grove have all fallen and the water has dried up in the well?" (or, in other words, while food is still plentiful). To this proposal Maku's father agreed, and told the groomsman to return after five days. Maku's father then consulted the headman, his assistant, and the *Jogmanjhi*, and having fixed a convenient day, they began to make preparations. When the groomsman returned, he found they had tied ten loop knots in a number of strings, which meant that the marriage was to take place after ten days. One of the knotted strings was sent to each person or to each family who were to be invited. They untied a knot every day, and when the last knot was untied they knew that the wedding-day had arrived. Manka's friends, on receiving the strings, sent out similar ones to their relatives and others whom they wished to invite The *Jogmanjhis* of Baromasia and of Taletandi then went round their respective villages to invite the people to erect in each village a booth or *mandwa* adjoining the houses of the bride and bridegroom. These booths, which were to be the chief scene of the wedding festivities, were constructed with great care according to a uniform pattern. In the centre was fixed a post made from a branch of the *mahua* tree (*Bassia latifolia*) and in a little hole at the foot of this post some grains of rice, three roots of turmeric, and five cowrie shells were buried, wrapped in a leaf of the *sal* tree. The post was then wound round with ropes of straw and smoothly plastered over with soft clay. It was then whitewashed, and rude pictures of date palms and human beings were painted upon it with charcoal and a kind of red ochre found in the hills and called *giru*. Posts were erected at four corners, and walls and a roof was constructed of leaf and branches of trees. The booth was decorated with festoons of mango leaves, which were also hung across the entrance to the house from the street. In three places strings with mango leaves intertwined were hung across the village street. Three fowls, two white and one brown, were sacrificed on the day the booth was erected and the young men who had helped to construct it were regaled with beer and cooked rice. *Dom* drummers were engaged by both parties. The booth in Taletandi having been completed, on the same evening the *Jogmanjhi* invited the villagers to assemble in it. The headman and his wife sat down on a mat, and three maidens anointed them with oil and turmeric. The village priest and his wife were anointed next, and last of all the bridegroom. Rice beer was served round, and the proceedings ended with a dance.

Three days later the ceremony known as the water marriage was performed by three women and two girls. One of the women, wearing a *sari* which was to be given as a present to Maku's mother, carried a drawn sword (in later times a stick was often substituted) and another wearing the cloth which was to be presented to Maku's grand-mother, wore the scabbard. A third woman, wearing the cloth intended for Maku's other grandmother, carried a bow and arrows. The two girls carried each a small water-pot, in which there were a few cowries, on the head. The *Jogmanjhi* joined the party, carrying a *lota* full of rice beer, some thread, three pointed arrows and a *kudali* or hoe. A procession was formed, headed by the *Dom* drummers, and proceeded to the nearest tank, the three women dancing all the way. One of the villagers, who was for the time being nicknamed the Brahmin, dug a miniature triangular tank with the hoe, and fixing an arrow upright in the ground at each corner wound the thread round them five times. The *Jogmanjhi* then marked the places on the ground where the arrows were inserted with red paint, and offered a libation of rice beer to the Great Spirit Marang Buru and the spirits of the dead village headmen, with the following prayer: "We salute thee, Marang Buru. Thou dost see that we marry and take away this water. Let no one be envious. Let no spell, charm, or hocus-pocus interfere with the success of this marriage." The three women and the two girls then entered the water. The woman with the bow shot an arrow into the water and she with the sword made a slash at it. The two girls dipped their water-pots simultaneously, and simultaneously raised them on to their heads and covered them with the cloth intended for Maku. The water pots were then carried in procession back to the village and carefully deposited in a safe place. Another miniature tank was dug at Manka's house, with arrows at the corners and thread wound round them. Two bullock-yokes were placed within it. On these Manka and his father took their stand, the latter directly in front of the former. A sword was placed flat on the father's head and on it was poured water, which flowed down to his son's head. Manka was then bathed by having water poured over him and a few grains of rice and a little *dhubi* grass wrapped up in *sal* leaves were tied to his wrist. About the same time a little rice and *dhubi* grass, with the addition of three pieces of turmeric root, wrapped in *mahua* leaves, were tied round Maku's wrist by her friends at Baromasia.

The time now arrived to set out for the bride's village, and a procession was formed headed by the *Dom* drummers. The groomsman carried five cloths in a basket, one for Maku's mother, two for her grandmothers, one for herself, and one for her youngest brother. Manka's father took two rupees with him, one as the balance of the *pon* still due, the other for the headman of Baromasia. He also took a goat, a good supply of rice beer, some rice, and also, as provision for the way, a quantity of cooked food. Arriving at the neighbourhood of Baromasia they halted under a tree and began to dance. Maku's friends, hearing of their approach, sent a water-pot of water and a *lota* to them, and then forming themselves into a procession, with *Dom* drummers, went on to meet them. The two processions danced towards each other, danced together for a time, and then halted for the exchange of salutations. Then they went dancing together down the village street, and at each house some raw sugar was put into Manka's mouth. Having made the round of the village, they returned to the spot where Manka's friends had first halted, and here Manka was again bathed and anointed with oil and turmeric. His hair was combed and dressed and he was arrayed in new garments, amid boisterous merriment Maku's party (called the *sariati*, while Manka's were the *bariati*) then returned to the house, and the *Jogmanjhi* soon summoned both parties to the *sindra dhan* or marking of the bride with red-lead. The *barati* assembled in front of the house. Manka's brother Chede with two other lads then entered the house, and after having been served with beer, carried out Maku, who was arrayed in her bridal garments and seated in a large new shallow basket. Manka was awaiting her, sitting astride the shoulder of one of his friends. Maku was raised up to his level, and each sprinkled the other three times with sprigs of a mango tree dipped in water. Relatives on both sides saluted each other. Some red-lead (*sindur*) in a *sal* leaf was then handed to Manka, who with the little finger of his right hand marked Maku five times on her forehead and then wiped the leaf on her brow. He then lifted her out of the basket and a corner of his *chadar* was tied to the corner of her *sari*. Maku's mother then brought out a brass plate upon which were a ball of cowdung, another of dough, some unhusked rice, a few pieces of *dhubi* grass, and some powdered turmeric. She made passes with this plate over the heads of the proud couple, and scattered the rice and g ass on the ground behind Manka's back. Then dipping her finger in flour and water she dabbed a little on his cheeks and he did the same to her. She put wristlets on him and threw the balls over his and her own backs. Other relatives made passes as she had done and dabbed more flour and water on Manka's cheeks. Fire in an earthenware cover of a water-pot was brought out, and Maku's mother and aunts made passes over it with the right hand, while holding a pestle used for husking rice in the left. The last to perform this ceremony broke the lid with a thrust of the pestle and the fire was quenched with water.

All now adjourned to the booth and circled three times round the central post. Manka and Maku sat down on a mat while maidens anointed them with oil and marked them again with red-lead. The groomsman and the girl who acted as bridesmaid and a few relatives were also anointed. The young couple were then conducted to the house, and fed on rice, milk, and raw sugar. The *bariati* then took possession of the booth, and sitting on straw chewed tobacco and talked in parables to the bride's friends. At length one of the latter said, "Come let us convert our bodies from baskets set on the ground into Palmyra palms." All then stood up, and saluted, and the *bariati* returned to their camp. After a short interval the *Jogmanjhi*, carrying a *lota* of water, summoned them "to come and gather potherbs." They returned to the bride's house, where a goat was killed with all the ceremonies already described, the libation being offered this time by Maku's father, who prayed that the young couple might not stumble or trip and that they might keep to the left hand or to the right hand of all the thorns in their path. The remaining rupee was paid to Maku's father through the medium of the groomsman, the cloths were presented to the women—who, according to etiquette, measured them and said they were too short—and the rupee was given to the headman of Baromasia, all with the accompaniment of beer-drinking, salutations, conundrums, and jokes. The *bariati* then returned to their camp and, having summoned the *Jogmanjhi*, asked him to inform the bride's father that, all the customs having been observed, they now wished to return home, taking the bride with them. The bride's father, in reply, sent the *Jogmanjhi* back to invite the *bariati* to the parting ceremonies. The *bariati* then came to the booth, where they began to dance. Manka and Maku were led out and all followed them to the end of the street, where the men and women of the bride's party drew up in two rows, and Manka's party, led by the groomsman, saluted them in turn, the near relatives of the newly-married pair standing apart and saluting each other in the prescribed form. One of Maku's friends then cried, "Come, friends, let us make this the shade of a *makua* tree" and all sat down. The spokesman of the bride's party then addressed the following speech to Manka's father; "Do not they say that we are following in the way our fathers trod, and do not they say that a certain Santal has chosen a pot out of twelve kilnsfull, by tapping and sounding it? Now this article has been made over by one man to another man, and he is responsible for it. Should it become a thief or immoral person, or blind or lame, the responsibility rests with him. Do they not also say that owing to the virtue of the house come sons and daughters-in-law? We shall teach them to cook, to bring water and leaves and firewood, and should they refuse to be taught then let us know and then shall we not all unite in instructing her? And friends, a certain Santal has from to-day sold even to bones and ashes, but the blood of the head and of the ears he has not sold; should blood be shed he will require it at your hands." More exhortations followed before the final salutations took place.

Manka's friends, on their return, were accompanied by five young men, relatives of Maku, and two elderly women. One of the men carried a rice-husking pestle, with the iron-bound end covered, and one woman a mat. The bridal couple were carried in an open palki. On reaching Taletandi, the party halted at the entrance to the street and began to dance. The *Jogmanjhi* of Taletandi then brought them drinking water, and Manka's mother came with water in one vessel and raw sugar in another and sat on the mat which the women had brought from Baromasia. Manka sat in her lap, and she first put raw sugar into his mouth and then gave him water to rinse it with.

Maku received the same treatment, and the procession went dancing down the street, the pair being fed with sugar at each house. When the headman's house was reached a libation of water was poured out to his predecessor's spirit. Having gone the round of the village, the party returned to the front of Manka's house, where his sister Maeno brought out water and washed first his and then Maku's feet. His mother again fed them both with sugar; made passes over them with a brass plate containing *dhubi* grass, dough, rice, turmeric, oil and an iron wristlet, the bride having added to these articles a small box containing red-lead and a comb she had brought with her from her own home; and dabbed a little flour and water on Maku's forehead. Maku did the same to her mother-in-law. Then the mother-in-law applied oil to the parting of Maku's hair and combed it and put red-lead along the whole length of the parting. Maku then combed her mother-in-law's hair and applied red-lead to the parting and repeated the process to five of Manka's aunts, paternal and maternal. Fire was brought out as at Baromasia, and similar passes made over it, the earthen lid being smashed in this case by one of the young men from Baromasia with the pestle he had brought for this purpose. Then the company adjourned to the booth, and the couple circled round the central post, and then sat on a mat while three maidens anointed them with oil and turmeric. They were then conducted to the house and fed on rice, milk, and raw sugar, and the young folks of the village danced in the booth till daylight. In the morning the young men from Baromasia received parched rice and were asked to cut off the head of the goat which was to be cooked for a feast. The floor of the booth was swept and smeared with cowdung, and Maeno drew pictures on it with flour and water.

Manka's mother then brought from the house a flat basket and was followed by two aunts, one carrying a *lota* of water, the other a small earthenware pot containing rice brought from Manka's home. All had rice in their laps as well. To the music of the drums, all five women danced into the booth, circled five times round the central post, and shook out the rice from their laps at the foot of it, depositing the other articles in convenient spots. A mat was spread over the pictures on the ground, and Manka and Maku sat upon it, while passes were made over the pot containing the rice from Maku's house with the last basket in which some rice and *dhubi* grass had been placed. The rice and grass were scattered on the ground behind the young couple's backs, and Manka's mother, having made passes over them with the basket, put a brass ornament on her daughter-in-law's neck. All the available aunts repeated the passes. Maeno, Manka's sister, then bathed the feet of the young couple, but in the case of Maku, having finished the washing, she seized both ankles firmly with her hands. The bystanders cried out to Maku's friend. "See a crab has seized her; to the rescue!" One of them at once gave a wrist ornament to the groomsman, which he gave to Maeno, who then released Maku. The young couple again went to the booth, circled five times round the pillar, and were about to re-enter the house when Maeno stood in their way and blocked the door. The groomsman gave Maeno four pice, and she let them in. Manka's mother thereupon emerged with the flat basket, followed by two aunts. All went dancing into the booth, circled five times round the pillar, and danced back to the house.

The feast was now ready. First the young men from Baromasia were served in the booth, after them all the other guests, and beer was supplied in leaf cups. Next morning Manka's father, accompanied by the headman and his assistant, took the young men from Baromasia out to the jungle where the cattle were feeding. Pointing out to them a bull-calf, he indicated that they were to receive it as a present. One of them slapped it on the back to signify their approval of the gift. The headman then said to them: "Come, ye brothers of the bride, will you not take the property away with you?" They replied: "Let it remain here a day or two." The headman then rejoined, "Should it fall into a pit or a ravine, or be eaten by jackals or leopards, or stolen away, the loss will be the bride's brothers'."

Hair washing was the next item in the programme. A soapy kind of earth was mixed with water, and Manka plastered a little of the mixture on Maku's forehead. She then washed his hair with the same soap, poured water over him, and anointed him with oil. Some of the women bathed and anointed Maku, who then washed her husband's feet. She and he saluted each other, and she proceeded to wash the feet of the village chief, his assistant, the priest, her uncles-in-law, the headman's wife, the assistant's wife, and all her aunts-in-law, maternal or paternal. After the washing she saluted and was saluted by each one of them. Then Manka's brother came, with his feet and legs swathed in straw. She removed this, washed his feet, and grasped his ankles. He offered her some jungle fruit to let him go. She disdainfully rejected the offer, and her brothers remarked that something more was required. Chede then offered four annas, which Maku accepted, and they poured water over each other. Maku then washed Maeno's feet and playing the crab again received a small ornament as a ransom. But Maeno had now to bathe Maku's feet, and it was Maku's turn to give a present to Maeno to gain her freedom. A salutation between Maku and Maeno brought this ceremony to an end.

All the company were then invited to enter the house, where they were served with rice beer by Manka and Maku. The guests sat round in a circle, and when the drinking was over the young couple sat in the centre while suitable exhortations regarding the duties of husband and wife were addressed to them. The address to the bridegroom was as follows: "Up till to-day you have been free to come and go. Wherever night overtook you, there you stayed till morning. Now, wherever you go, you must return home at night. We have bound a wooden bell around your neck as we do to straying cattle. You must shake this and make it sound. If you go to a dance, go together; and if it is dark, come home together. If you are ill or suffer pain, tell each other about it. Help your wife to bring home firewood and leaves for plates. If you go hunting and find fruit, eat half and bring home half to your wife. If you get part of an animal slain, eat a portion of it and, wrapping the rest in leaves, bring it home to your wife. At all times and in every way help each other, and do not be separated from each other." To Maku, the homily was in the following terms :—" Now bride, we have to-day put you in subjection to this youth. Whenever he comes home, meet him with a *lota* of water. Whenever he calls you, go at once. If you become tired of this place, tell him so, 'Come. I am tired of this place, let us visit my father and mother.' But do not run away with anybody. When you go to the jungle for firewood and leaves, call to him to go with you. Do not go alone. From to-day you are mates; love each other and live in peace."

Food was served out again, Maku handing round the rice and Manka the relish. The young men of Taletandi then anointed the "bride's brothers," combed and dressed their hair, and painted their eyelids with lamp-black. Hand in hand they went to the booth and had a farewell dance. Maku saluted her brothers and the two women who accompanied her, and they set out for home. Maku followed them weeping and the village girls followed her with words of consolation. "They will return in a few days" they said: "This is the lot of girls; what can you do?"

The young men of Taletandi then pulled down the booth, throwing the central post and the twine into a tank. The rice and turmeric roots which had been buried at the foot of this post and the similar articles which had been tied round the wrists of Manka and Maku were carefully examined to see if they showed any signs of sprouting. If they did, it was a sign that the marriage was to be fruitful and prosperous. To the great satisfaction of the old wives, the rice buried in the booth was found to be germinating. The young men and women danced till after sunset when a quantity of liquor called "dew beer" was supplied to them. A supper which followed brought the festivities to an end.

Five days later the groomsman and two of the "bride's brothers," coming to Manka's house, were regaled with rice beer and pork—a pig being killed in their honour. Next day they conducted Manka and Maku and three of their friends back to Baromasia, where the *Jogmanjhi* invited the villagers to meet them and to drink beer in their honour. Next day the pair were conducted back to Taletandi, where the *Jogmanjhi* again officiated at a beer drinking to celebrate their return and to shew hospitality to their friends.

Although there had been a good many presents given, in most cases others were given in exchange and in this respect the balance in the end was about even. Maku's father was expected to present gifts to Manka's in proportion to the *pon* he received. In this case he gave a brass cup and plate, and a cow with a calf. Nearly all the relatives of the bride received gifts from Manka's father, but they gave something in return.

A few days after Maku's arrival in her new home, the women of Taletandi told her she must be married to the spring from which they drew their water, to propitiate the demon. This spirit of the well was the women's demon: they had to gratify him so that the water would not cause disease and children would not fall in and be drowned. So Maku took a water-pot on her head and some red-lead in her hand, and going to the spring she made five marks with the paint on its margin, opposite the point where the sun rose, at the same time saying: "From to-day I shall draw water here and drink it. May it not give me headache or stomach-ache. Although I come to draw water at midnight, may there be nothing to make me afraid." Then she filled her pot and carried it home. Manka's friends all spoke of Maku as "Our bride." She was family property, bought by family funds. Manka's mother took her in hand to teach her her new duties, and her happiness depended more upon her mother-in-law's good-will than upon her husband's.

CHAPTER VII.

THE SANTAL REBELLION.

TO the reader of the previous chapters, the life led by Manka and his friends may appear to be idyllic in its natural simplicity and peacefulness; and probably the same impression would have been made upon a casual observer of the actual facts. But there was a skeleton in the cupboard. This was Behari Modi, shop-keeper and moneylender, of Dokanpur. He was only a skeleton metaphorically; in reality, his bones were exceptionally well-padded with adipose tissue, and his girth was as ample as his income. Nearly every Santal, like almost every other small cultivator in India, has his *mahajan* who finances him, advancing him seed in the sowing season, and food for the interval that is to follow, and receiving repayment with heavy interest at the harvest. Old Manka was easy going, ignorant of accounts, and improvident. He little recked that year by year the balance against him in Behari's books was increasing, in spite of the fact that he had repaid in interest alone a sum equivalent to at least twice the principal. It was Behari Modi who had provided the rice for the feasting and beer-drinking at the naming and at the *Chatiar* ceremonies, and when application was made to him for the wherewithal to celebrate Manka's wedding, the benevolent money-lender professed to be moved with compassion for his creditor, and offered him twenty-five rupees, free of interest, on the condition that he, his son, and grandson were to work for him, and for him alone, till this advance, and both the principal and interest that had already accumulated, were paid up. The bait was swallowed, and all the family were firmly fixed by the money-lender's hook. Struggle as they might, they would only make their servitude the more sure. A bond was executed, old Manka affixing a rude attempt at an arrow-head as his mark, and it was duly attested by witnesses. It was not until 1860 that a deed of this nature was declared to be illegal, although in an enactment of 1843 (Act V) the existence of this form of serfdom was recognised; and in spite of the Act of 1860 there are thousands of cultivators in Bengal and Bihar to-day who are for all practical purposes the slaves of the money-lenders. They do not know that their bondage is unlawful, and, even if they did, many of them would not seek deliverance from it. They know that as long as they are bond-servants it is their owners' interest to keep them alive, and that is the bound of their earthly ambition. From that day neither old Manka, his son, nor his grandson had a thing he could call his own, except his soul, about which he knew very little and cared less. They ploughed and they sowed, they reaped and they mowed, for Behari Modi, who left them just sufficient grain for their food, with a little extra to obtain cloth by barter, but nothing more. Their cattle were the money-lender's, including both their produce and their labour. Their land they held only nominally. When young Manka's father gave a cow as a present to the "bride's brothers" at the marriage, it was added to the family debt. If the worm threatened to turn, the threat of an appeal to court, with the certainty of a decree in favour of the money-lender, enabling him to sell them up to the last pice, and turn them out of their home, was always sufficient to ensure submission.

Soon after Manka's marriage, numbers of Santals went off to work on the new railway that was under construction. There was work for all, men, women and children, in digging and carrying earth for the embankments, and it was work at which the Santals excelled. It was piece-work, too, and a family, by working hard during their own slack season, from January till June, could earn what to them was wealth. Whole parties marched off to the music of their flutes and came back fat and sleek, shining with oil and loaded with cloth and brass ornaments. Young Manka, whose fetters were beginning to gall, conceived the idea of going off with the next procession, and communicated the project to his father. By working hard for a year or two, could they not save enough to pay their debts and regain their freedom? The father approved, and arrangements were made for Manka and Maku's departure for Eldorado. But Behari Modi got wind of their intent and intervened with an absolute veto. That his debtor should pay up in full was the last thing he wished for. He had got them cheap, and he meant to keep them. So there was nothing for it but to obey. Had it been some thirty years later, Manka might have put himself into the hands of a coolie recruiter, who would have smuggled him off to Assam under an assumed name; but that loophole of escape was not available in his young days.

Then there were the police. Two illustrations of their methods must suffice, for the subject in a large one. Goats and fowls had been disappearing in rapid succession from Manka's courtyard by night. In the neighbourhood there was a village of Dusadhs, who were all born thieves. Manka's father went to them, and charged them with the theft. "And do you really think", said they, "that we are going to pay the police two rupees a month for nothing?" Their compact with the custodians of the public peace simply was that they, the police, should leave them, the Dusadhs, alone during the dark nights of the month. Then one morning, a dead pilgrim, who had been on his way to Deoghur, was found lying in the village street. He was old and emaciated and had evidently died of exhaustion and exposure. Word was sent to the police, and the sub-inspector or *daroga* came in person to investigate. Manka's house was nearest to the spot where the body lay; so the *daroga* informed the inmates that if they did not pay him ten rupees down, he would prove that they had murdered and robbed the pilgrim. "How can you do that?" they asked. "By battering in his head with a stick, and testifying that I found the blood-stained stick and some clothes and money concealed in your house." "But you have no witness to prove that we did it." "More than you have to prove you did not." So application had to be made to Behari Modi. He paid the money not so very unwillingly. It was the cheapest way out of the difficulty. It would have been a serious loss if Manka's people had been imprisoned, and if once the case had got into Court more than the police would have had to be squared, and at a higher figure than ten rupees, to prove that the innocent were not guilty. Then the ten rupees were always an additional rivet in the fetters. Why did people oppressed in this way not appeal to the Magistrate? Because they could not afford it. To gain access to him personally his servants would have to be bribed. To get a petition presented, the palms of the court clerks would have to be greased. It was a very simple trick, in assorting the petitions, to leave those for which a private fee had not been paid permanently at the bottom of the pile.

The landlord was another natural enemy. The people of Taletandi, or their fathers, had reclaimed from jungle every square foot of their arable land, and they felt it to be an injustice that all the increment went to the man who had done nothing to earn it. There was no survey or assessment; leases and even receipts were unknown. When a man paid his rent he went home and tied a knot in a string,—that was the only record. Every now and then the landlord clapped on four annas to the rupee. He also took a goat, a pot of ghee, and a rupee from each house at the time of the Durga Puja, and additional levies were made on the occasion of marriages, funerals, and other social events in his family circle. He also claimed the right of taking possession of any of their live stock at half their market value, and the people considered themselves lucky if even this was paid. Then the ryots had also to feed a small army of the landlord's retainers whenever they received visits from them, which was very frequently. It was Behari Modi who paid old Manka's rent out of the crops, and he always saw that it was made the first charge upon them; but the vexations the whole system of land tenure caused were felt throughout the village.

A year or so after his marriage, towards the end of the hot season of 1855, Manka took his bride to pay a prolonged visit to her parents in the Daman-i-Koh. They found their friends there in a state of ferment. It is true they were in some respects better off in the Daman than were their fellow tribesmen who lived outside it, as they were Government tenants. But all the privileges enjoyed by the Paharias were not shared by the Santals. The former had a monopoly, rent free, of the fertile lands on the flat hilltops. They were not under the jurisdiction of the law courts (except in cases of the gravest crimes) but had a hill assembly of their own chiefs to try them; and their *Sardars* or overseers, their *Naibs* or Deputies, and the *Manjhis* or village headmen, received stipends to the extent of Rs. 15,000 per annum in the aggregate, for keeping the peace. Proximity to these highly favoured people, who were still notorious thieves, and grossly abused their many privileges, no doubt aggravated the honest and industrious Santals' feelings of exasperation on account of the evils they were subject to. The traders, too, had followed the stream of Santal immigration into the Daman and fed in green pastures along its banks. They bought from the Santals with one set of weights and sold to them with another—both sets being spurious; they used measures with false bottoms and with thick lining, and in this and similar ways they robbed the cultivators of the bulk of their hard-earned produce. The Santals are always dreaming of a time when they dwelt secure, masters of the soil their own labour had made productive, and free to cut and hack the jungle till the jungle was no more. From time to time a tide of race feeling sweeps over the people, making them very susceptible to any agitators or wonderworkers who hold out to them the prospect of a renewal of their pristine prosperity. To some extent, such a movement seems to have been on foot in 1855, contributing to the general feeling of unrest and discontent.

It is said that the Santals made representations regarding their grievances both to the local authorities and to the Commissioner, but it is also said that there is no record that the petitions ever reached their destinations. It is admitted, however, that the Government generally was culpably ignorant of the trend of affairs in the Santal country. It was a matter of self-gratulation to them that so much jungle had been reclaimed and that the revenue of the Daman had in a few years been raised from a minus quantity to Rs. 80,000. But their interest in the matter seems to have ended there.

In the village of Bagnadihi there was an uncle of Maku's father, Chumar by name, who had four sons, Sido, Kanhu, Chand and Bairab. When Manka and Maku visited them these sons assured them that Marang Buru, the Great Spirit, had appeared to them seven times on seven successtive days in divers forms. He was seen first as a cloud descending from heaven; then as a tongue of fire with a knife glowing in the midst; then as a mysterious veiled figure; then as a shadow in the bright sunshine where no shadow should be; then as a *sal* tree suddenly springing from barren ground, and finally as a white man clothed in a loin-cloth. They also said that Marang Buru gave them a sacred book, wherein was nothing written. Manka knew that blank slips of paper, which were said to be leaves from this book, had been circulating among the villages. This, the brothers said, was being done by the Great Spirit's command, to prepare the people for what was to follow.

Manka and Maku returned to Baromasia. On the 15th June, a messenger arrived there, bringing a *sal* branch with ten leaves upon it. He mentioned the name of a village near Barhait, the capital of the Daman, and passed on. Ten days later, nearly all the villagers set out for this appointed place, and as they drew near it they saw bands like their own moving towards the common centre, as if drawn by invisible wires. Thousands were rallying round Sido and Kanhu, not only from every part of the Daman, but from Birbhum, Bhagalpur, Hazaribagh, and Manbhum as well. Several davs were spent in discussion, and on June 30th an ultimatum (which, it is said, was never received) was despatched to the Supreme Government as well as to local officials.

Then the march began. What its definite object in the first place was—if there was any—has always been obscure, but afterwards the leaders declared that their sole purpose was to march in a body to Calcutta in the hope that by a personal interview with the Governor-General they would secure the relief they had sought in vain elsewhere. Certain it is that at first they were accompanied by their women and children, and that the gathering generally was more of a festive than a warlike character. This at least was true as long as food supplies held out. After that, in spite of the efforts of the leaders, who wished to appeal for public subscriptions, there was a good deal of plundering. The spark that set the heather on fire was struck at a village called Pachkattia on 7th July. A sub-inspector of police, Mohesh by name, who was also a rent-collector, was bribed by the Hindu usurers, who were now alarmed at the aspect affairs had assumed, to arrest Sido and Kanhu on a false charge of burglary. He proceeded to the Santal camp accompanied by a party of constables, or *barkandazes* (matchlock-men) as they were then called and taking with him a cartload of ropes. Confronted by a larger and more determined looking gathering than he had anticipated, he thought better of his purpose, and said that his object was to investigate a reported case of snake-bite. The Santals told him he was not a *daroga* but a decoit, and when their leaders asked him to promise to levy a contribution from every householder in his jurisdiction for the support of the expedition, he agreed, and took his departure. Then Sido and Kanhu were informed what the real object of his visit had been. They recalled Mohesh, who after some equivocation confessed his design. "If you have any charge against us arrest us now," said Sido. Mohesh foolishly ordered his men to seize and bind Sido and Kanhu. Thereupon the Santals fell upon and overpowered the police party. After a hurried trial, Sido slew Mohesh with his own hand and nine of the constables were also left dead upon the field.

That was the beginning of the rebellion. For a fortnight at least the Santals were left free to devastate the country right and left. Their cry was "Death to the money-lenders, the police, the civil court officers, the landlords, and the railway subordinates." The first European to reach the scene of the disturbance was Mr. James Pontet, who had been superintendent of the Daman-i-Koh since 1836, charged specially with the duty of settling the Santals in the valleys. A just and conscientious officer, straightforward and of clean hands in all his dealings with the people, "Ponteen", as they called him, was revered by the Santals and in spite of endless red tape and official worry he had accomplished good results in his district. The Santal leaders refused to let their followers, who had now tasted blood and were thirsting for more, lay hands on him but had him carried off to a safe retreat where he was secure from harm but unable to communicate with his superiors.

In those days many an old score was wiped out. An arch-enemy of the Daman Santals was Sumar Singh, the Paharia Raja of Sankora. In his father's time, the raj had by some mistake been included in the Daman, and had stipends assigned to it. Sire and son had raided and plundered their neighbours on every hand and then pleaded their privileges as Paharias to escape the consequences. This same family, by the way, came into prominence again in 1868 when in order to avert the sale and extinction of their raj, they seized an unfortunate Bhojpur trader and sacrificed him upon the summit of their highest hill. Sumar Singh had made himself particularly obnoxious to the Santals and they determined to settle with him at last. But natural death anticipated murder. Less fortunate was the *zemindar* of Narainpur who, like many of his class, seems to have been also a money-lender. It was and still is the custom to pay rent by *kistis* or instalments, and quittance in full is called *farkati*. The insurgents seized this old gentleman, and with fiendish humour, cried "Four annas" as they cut off his legs at the knee, "Eight annas" as they severed the thighs, "Twelve annas" as they amputated the arms, and "*Farkati*" as they hewed off his head. Another landlord, when the Santals set fire to his house, sought refuge in a tank. The rebels fired arrows at him till his head was like a well-filled quiver. Then, dragging his dead body from the water and laying it on a large stone, they chopped it into twenty-two pieces—"one for each of his ancestors," they said. The stone is still pointed out, and until a few years ago the victim's two widows were living in the neighbourhood of the murder.

The marauders were indeed formidable bands. Sido and Kanhu's followers alone numbered 30,000. Their brothers Chand and Bairab also joined them, and all over the country were smaller gangs, who, casting all pretence of moderation to the winds, stole and murdered at their will. It was a hard time for money-lenders and landlords, and all the minions of the law. For once at least the tables were turned, and the biters were bitten; the oppressors had returned into their bosoms good measure, pressed down, well shaken, and running over. The whirlwind they had sown swept down upon them without pity or remorse. The men of Taletandi made Behari Modi their first but not their only victim, and burnt his house, with all its precious accounts and documents, to ashes. Several Europeans, chiefly among the indigo planting community, were also slain. One European, mounted on an elephant, with his two sons on horseback, all armed with guns, went out to fight a party of Santals. All three were killed, by arrows. At Sahebgunge, a European family, driven to take refuge in a boat, kept up a destructive fire upon their assailants, while keeping beyond the range of the latter's arrows. It is said that two English ladies were among the victims, but only one of the Santal leaders showed any animosity against Europeans, except when attacked. The others said consistently throughout that they had no quarrel with the British Government but only with their Bengali oppressors, and that all they wanted from the latter was justice and fairplay.

So unexpected was the outbreak, that there were not at the time 1,200 troops within 80 miles of the scene. The first regular engagement was at Pirpainti, before the end of July, where the Bhagalpur Hill Rangers, as the PaliariaCorps first organised by Cleveland were called, were routed by the rebels, and this was not the only occasion when they were victorious over regulars. Then Major Jervis,—whose personal narrative of the events he took part in, communicated to Sir William Hunter thirteen years afterwards, is the most vivid account of the rebellion that has seen the light of publicity,—was ordered up from Barrackpur with a detachment of sepoys. Proceeding by train to Raniganj, they marched two days and a night amid pouring rain, to Suri, the capital of Birbhum, where rumours of an impending attack had caused a panic in the bazar and led the officials to fortify the jail. In all the villages along the line of march the shopkeepers welcomed the troops with tears and forced sweetmeats and parched rice upon them.

Still the Government, anxious to avoid the appearance of being alarmed, and guided by the reports of its district officials who tried to minimise the gravity of the outbreak, placed the military under the control of the civilians in charge of the affected districts. The result was endless bickerings and no improvement in the situation. About 25th July General Lloyd was despatched with fuller powers, but these were again curtailed. The planters then offered their services as a body, and His Highness of Murshidabad supplied elephants for transport. On 15th August a proclamation was issued, offering a free pardon to all who should give themselves up by a certain date, except the ringleaders and those who were guilty of murder. This offer was ignored, or scornfully rejected, and the rebellion, which had now assumed the character of a guerilla war, dragged on for another month. "It was not war," Major Jervis said; "it was execution," and he added that there was not a sepoy employed who did not often feel ashamed of himself. The troops would surround a village, and call upon its inhabitants to surrender. On one occasion forty-five men took refuge in a mud hut. The magistrate who accompanied the troops, summoned them to surrender. The only reply was a shower of arrows from the half opened door. "Mr. Magistrate," said the Major, "this is no place for you," and leading up his sepoys he made them cut a large hole in the wall. He shouted in to the rebels that if they did not surrender he would fire in upon them. Again a volley of arrows was the reply. The sepoys advanced and fired repeatedly and were as often fired upon in return. After every volley, quarter was offered, but probably the Santals had no idea what was meant. At last the Major, anxious to save some of the foe alive if possible, rushed the hut. A single old man, dabbled with blood, standing erect among the corpses, was the only survivor. When a sepoy went up to him, calling on him to lay down his arms, the old man, rushing upon him, hewed him down with his battle axe. Major Jervis afterwards declared that the Santals he had to fight against were the most truthful set of men he had ever met, and brave to infatuation. Their humble military equipment did not include the white flag; they did not know how to give in. As long as their drums beat, they would stand, and allow themselves to be shot down; when their drums were silenced, they would move away about a quarter of a mile, form up again, and wait till a few more volleys were fired into them. A Lieutenant under Major Jervis had once to shoot down seventy five men before the drums ceased and the party fell back. Few prisoners were taken except wounded men, who upbraided the English officers for taking the side of their oppressors. On September 24th the Magistrate of Birbhum reported that during the previous fortnight upwards of thirty villages had been plundered, and that the whole district to within a short distance of Deoghur was in the hands of the rebels, who were now formed into two large bodies each from 12,000 to 14,000 strong. The mails were stopped and the inhabitants had deserted the villages and fled One of these bands, under Seru Manjhi, was encamped six miles west of Suri, where it had thrown up earth works and entrenched against attack. With a refinement of chivalry the Santal rebels sometimes gave warning of their intention to attack a certain place. Thus a day or two before the last-mentioned date, Suri had again been thrown into a state of panic when the post runner to Deoghur returned saying the rebels under Seru Manjhi had seized him, stolen the mails, and spared his life only on the condition that he should carry back to the Magistrate of Suri a *sal* branch with three leaves on it as a sign that the place would be attacked in three days. This assault did not come off, probably because in the meantime Seru Manjhi's attention had been diverted by the news of a serious disaster to the northern army of rebels. At Sagrampur, on the borders of Monghyr and Bhagalpur, the Bhagalpur Hill Rangers, under Captain Fagan, inflicted upon the Santals a defeat so terrible that the surrounding villagers who had taken no part in the rising deserted their homes and fled panic-stricken to the hills. Still the Santals fought on, refusing to yield. In October, the fact that some Brahmin priests were taken prisoners and carried off to celebrate the Durga Puja in the jungles was taken to indicate that some of the semi-Hinduized aborigines had joined the rebels.

CHAPTER VIII.

THE SANTAL REBELLION AND AFTER.

At last, early in November, Government reluctantly proclaimed martial law throughout the disturbed districts; 14,000 troops were employed, under General Lloyd and Brigadier-General Bird, to form a cordon round the rebels and sweep the jungles clear. The people still speak of an officer whose one command, when told that a rebel was caught, was *Katl karo*—"Execute." The hanging of Sido at Barhait, after a summary trial, in the presence of Mr. Pontet and a vast concourse of Santals, was the closing scene in the tragedy. The other leaders were exiled. Ten thousand Santals are said to have perished in the fighting. As the result of the inevitable official inquiry that followed, Mr. Pontet was severely censured and removed from office. He died broken-hearted in 1857. It is now generally recognised that he was a convenient scapegoat. Neglect on the part of his superiors was really responsible for the disaster of which he had to bear the blame.

Under the promise of redress the storm subsided as suddenly as it had arisen. Less than two years later, when the sepoy regiments that had been stationed in the Santal country—at Dumka, Deoghur, Rohini, and Baunsi—on account of the rising, were themselves infected with the spirit of the Mutiny and became openly insubordinate, the Santals proved so unswervingly loyal that a suggestion made to Government by a local official that a special police force should be enrolled from among them was successfully carried into effect. Soon afterwards the force of Paharia Hill Rangers was disbanded, in consequence of the reorganisation of the Native Army after the Mutiny. A few old pensioners are still to be found among their native hills.

Manka, who had passed through the rebellion unscathed, and without having incurred the guilt of bloodshed, except in fair fight, returned to a home at Taletandi no longer darkened by the dismal shadow of Behari Modi. One night he and his companions were encamped under a tree on the banks of the Ajai River after a day's hunting. They were roused from their sleep by the characteristic grunt of palki-bearers, and saw a palki being borne along in hot haste with sixteen *Kahars* to carry it in relays. By the light of the flaring torches they saw that it contained a pale-faced European lady, who was clasping a child to her breast and urging the bearers to increase their speed. Seeing the Santals, the bearers shouted to them "Come and help us across the river." As they ran along with them Manka learned that the lady was the wife of Mr. R. E. Ranald the Assistant Commissioner at Deoghur, where the 32nd Native Infantry were still stationed. Seeing how things were tending, he had sent off his wife and child by palki to Raniganj, the nearest railway station—sixty miles as the crow flies. It was October and the Ajai River was still fairly full of water. The palki-bearers said they could only venture to cross if the Santals led the way. Manka, feeling the way with his stick and never lifting his feet from the bottom lest the current should carry him away, carefully piloted them through ragged rocks and treacherous quicksands. The water at the deepest part almost reached his chin, and the palki-bearers had to put the palki on their heads and all hold on together: but at last they got safely through. Mr. Ranald remained at his post and was murdered, along with Lieutenant Cooper. There was a party of three dining together in the officers' quarters on the 9th October. The third was Lieutenant Rannie, whom the mutineers summoned to come out of the room before they killed his companions, and whom they spared, although he was a comparative stranger to the regiment. Like so many of the officers who fell during the Mutiny, Lieutenant Cooper had been particularly devoted to the men by whose hands he was murdered.

The result of the Santal Rebellion was that the Santals' grievances were so fully redressed that some of the newspapers of the day complained that the Government were encouraging rebellion by granting everything the rebels had asked for. The formation of the Santal Parganas, a district of 5,500 square miles, taken from Bhagalpur and Birbhum, with its headquarters first at Deoghur and afterward at Dumka, was one definite administrative change that dates from the close of the rebellion. The Parganas were made throughout a non regulation district, and Mr. Ashley Eden was the first Deputy Commissioner to be placed in charge. The system adopted was to utilise as far as possible the indigenous form of village organisation—the result, it has been said, of the lesson in government which had been taught not by the Government to a subject people, but by the subject people to its Government. The district was withdrawn to a large extent from the control of the law courts and the police, and in every village the headman, elected by the people and not only holding the office *ad vitam aut culpam* but bequeathing it to his son, was on a small scale magistrate, police officer, and revenue collector in one. Special provisions were made, at that or a later date, against serfdom, excessive usury, unjust enhancement of rent, and the permanent alienation of land. The usurers and traders were located in bazaars, each with an elected *chowdry* or mayor, whose functions were similar to those of the *mañjhi* among the Santals. So great is the change that has been brought about in the social relations of the various sections of the community that cases have been known where the Hindu and Mahomedan traders have elected a neighbouring Santal headman to be their *chowdry* when a vacancy occurred. The system has never been fully developed and it has all along been more or less a subject of official controversy, but to many who have had the best opportunities of observing its actual working its success has seemed so marked as to justify its application not only to all the 11,000 villages of the Santal Parganas but to a much wider area as well.

The *hul*, as it was and is still called, made a deep impression upon the imaginative minds of the Santal people. Old Manka, his son, and grandson, and young Manka's father-in-law and a host of other relatives by marriage were all "out" and all laid up a stock of stories to tell to future generations. Manka's father thenceforth reckoned his age by saying that his youngest son was married a year or two before the *hul*, and to the end of his life if Manka himself was asked how old he was he would say that his first child (named Budhu, after his grandfather) was born during the rice harvest following the end of the *hul*.

It may be as well to mention here the other principal agitations of a more public kind of which Manka was in his lifetime a spectator or in which he participated.

There was a threatened rising in 1871, when at one time it was rumoured that a large force of Santals was marching on Dumka. Rent was the main difficulty, the landlords always exercising remarkable ingenuity in evading the provisions of the laws that were supposed to control it. From time immemorial the Santals had had free use of the much valued mahua trees in their respective village lands. The landlords had begun to charge rent for these, and when the ryots refused to pay, the trees were cut down and sold as timber. This, in the eyes of the villagers, was about as gross an act of desecration as a landlord could commit, for the mahua tree with its edible flowers was above all the trees of the jungle the friend of the poor. This agitation merged into that caused by the Census of 1872. The authorities, foreseeing that an inquiry of this kind would probably be regarded with suspicion (What design has the Government, they would ask, in wanting to know how many unmarried daughters we have?) had taken the precaution of arranging to make the enumeration among the Santals through their own headmen and by a method in accordance with their own customs and ideas. Differently coloured threads were given to each headman,—black for men, red for women, white for boys, yellow for girls,—and all he had to do was to hand in one of these threads with a knot tied on it, for each individual. Little actual disturbance took place, but another impulse was given to protective legislation.

Trouble seemed to be brewing again about ten years later. The arrangements for the Census were again being made, and former fears were found to be not altogether removed. But the chief cause of anxiety was a movement of a socio religious kind which, from a head centre in Hazaribagh, affected to some degree the entire Santal community. Dub Babaji was a *yogi* of the kind very common in India, but in some way or other he managed to catch the mental eye of the Santal. He professed to live entirely on grass, which he ate like a cow; he wore nothing but wood and iron. He claimed to be an incarnation of the Deity, come to earth for the express purpose of persuading Santals to put away unclean animals like fowls and pigs from among them. This claim was attested by miracles, seen or reported. A mango slip planted one evening grow into a tree fifteen feet high before morning. Rifle bullets glanced harmlessly from the Babaji's breast, and a regiment of artillery had retired discomfited from before him. Those who disobeyed his commands perished miserably. A man who tried to plough with cows became stone blind. Another who went hunting fell dead when he discharged his arrow at the parrot—for the parrot was the Babaji. Stories like these soon reached Taletandi, and were followed by a stream of letters written in a small cramped hand on scraps of brown paper summoning the people to present themselves to the Babaji. The messengers who brought these missives urged the people without delay to kill their pigs and fowls, to give up demon worship, dancing, and drinking, and generally to conform to the customs of the Hindus. They were told that if they did not obey a deluge of fire rain would destroy them during the celebration of the approaching Durga Puja. The Santals furnish a receptive soil for this kind of seed, and many of the Taletandi people slaughtered their fowls and pigs forthwith. Others who did not do so were so worked upon by the predictions of evil that on the great day of the Durga Puja they kept their cattle and their children indoors from morning till night, determined to perish together.

Manka and his father resolved to visit the Babaji to see and hear for themselves before making up their minds to adopt the new teaching. On their way they passed through Madhupur where they found a force of 4,500 cavairy and infantry in camp, with a large body of police as well. It was the "Santal Field

Force," under General Sir Tom Gordon, which had been marched into the district on account of the disturbances. There had been rioting at Jamtara, where the Magistrate's bungalow was burned down, and elsewhere. Arriving at the Babaji's camp, they found him surrounded by a large concourse of enthusiastic followers, not only of Santals but of Kurmbis as well. The latter are a caste of cultivators, evidently an aboriginal tribe who have become semi-Hinduised, but they still retain some signs of their former status. Like the Santals they keep pigs and fowls, and occasionally a Santal man has married a Kurmbi woman and been allowed to compound the matter and retain both his wife and his position by furnishing a feast. The Babaji was directing his reforming energies to these Kurmbis as well as to the Santals, and there was some prospect that the reformed Kurmbis and Santals would coalesce to form a new caste of Hinduism. Manka and the other newcomers were at once pounced upon by the disciples of the Babaji and offerings of money were demanded from them. Each gave a few annas, and a meal of cooked food was supplied to each of them. They were then taken into the presence of the holy man, and water in which he had dipped his feet was sprinkled over them. They were exhorted to reverence the cow as sacred, to worship the goddess Kali and sacrifice to her, and to hold themselves aloof from all Santals and others who should refuse to do the same. Such people should not be allowed even to enter their houses, and eating or intermarrying with them was absolutely forbidden. The familiar injunctions to kill their fowls and pigs and to abstain from liquor and dancing were repeated, and the further advice was given that they should either destroy or throw away all the earthen pots and bamboo baskets or other household utensils which they had been using in their days of defilement and provide themselves with new ones. They were henceforth to regard themselves as *sapha horko* or pure persons. Further instructions regarding social customs and religious ceremonies would be given them by the Babaji at a great festival he was going to hold early in the approaching hot season. Manka and his friends retired, and meeting with acquaintances from their own neighbourhood they camped together for the night with the intention of setting out in the morning for their homes where they were diligently to practise the new faith and preach it as well. In the morning, however, the whole assembly was thrown into a state of consternation by the arrival of a large body of police, with a warrant for the arrest of the Babaji, signed by the Deputy Commissioner of the Santal Parganas, who had reason to believe that he was to some extent implicated in, if not directly responsible for, the recent riots. No opposition was offered, as every one was taken completely by surprise. When taken into custody the Babaji was found to have a sum of two thousand rupees in cash in his possession, and immense quantities of rice, *ghi*, and other food stuffs were also brought to light. These were evidently the offerings of his followers. This ignominious termination of the prophet's career completely dissipated his claim to supernatural powers, and it also scattered his disciples like chaff before the wind. Whatever hopes were cherished that this religious movement would act as a lever to raise the Santal people to the former prosperity of which they dreamed, were dashed to the ground. Here and there a stray individual still professed to be a *sapha hor*, but generally speaking the agitation soon flickered out, and left the tribe much as it had found them. Manka returned to his home a little wiser than when he left it, but not much sadder: for he had always regarded the movement with some misgivings, and was sincerely thankful that he had not slaughtered his pigs and fowls.

Note.—For the historical portions of the above narrative the writer wishes to express his indebtedness to Hunter's *Annals of Rural Bengal;* Carstairs' *Human Nature in Rural Bengal;* Bradley Birt's, *Story of an Inland Upland,* and a pamphlet entitled, *Some Historical and Ethnical Aspects of the Burdwan District,* by W. B. Oldham, printed for private circulation in 1894. These have been supplemented by materials from original sources, including personal interviews with individuals who themselves witnessed or took part in the events described.

CHAPTER IX.

THE CYCLE OF THE SEASONS.

MANKA and Maku were now a middle-aged couple, with a family of six. Manka stood five feet seven inches high, and weighed eight stones. His face was of the blubbery type, somewhat "dour" in repose, but pleasant and good-natured looking when lit up by a smile. His hair was thick, black, and long, and was well oiled; and he wore a poor apology for a beard. His figure was more sturdy than graceful, but in muscular development he might have sat as a model of Hercules. Maku had been a lissome lass, and still carried well the added weight of matronhood. Waterpots on the head had given her an erect carriage, and hard work, an open air life, simple diet, kept her supple and wiry beyond the usual term. In addition to the inevitable years, she bore a voluntary burden of heavy brass ornaments, on neck, wrists, and ankles, weighing in all at least twenty pounds.

Space forbids us to follow them through life in detail, but the present chapter will chronicle the events of a typical year.

The first event of importance was the *Sohrae* festival, a sort of Harvest Home, celebrated at the beginning of January, when the winter crops had all been gathered in. It was a saturnalia, a bout of drinking, dancing, and general debauchery, when the decorum and decency of routine life were for the time suspended. It was the rule, however, that when every other man got drunk, the *jogmañjhi* had to keep sober. In Manka's young days, the festival was inordinately prolonged, as it was held in rotation in the different villages; but latterly a rule was made by the district officials that it must be held if not simultaneously at least within a prescribed time. In preparation for the festival rice for brewing beer and a fowl for sacrifice were contributed by each family in the village. On the eve of the feast the village officials and other old men, assembling at the *manjhithan*, made a covenant to put earth on their eyes and cotton in their ears, that they might not see or hear what others did or said till the *Sohrae* was over. There was dancing that evening, but the serious work of the feast began next day A piece of ground was levelled, smoothed, and smeared with cowdung. Then squares were marked out with flour and water, from north to south. The people having bathed, the village priest, sitting with his face to the East, and with his left leg bent under him, began sacrifice. The first sacrifice was offered to *Jaherera*. *Jaher* is the sacred grove of *Sal* trees, and Jaher may be a forgotten god'et, and *Jaherera* his wife. An egg was placed in the first square, the four corners were marked with red-lead, and rice was scattered in the centre. Taking hold of a brown hen, the priest marked its head with red lead and fed it on the rice in the square. He then prayed, reminding the deity of the expense and trouble to which the poor people were put in worshipping it, claiming its favour and protection, and scolding it in unmeasured terms for previous neglect. Then by means of an axe held on the ground with its edge upright, he sawed partially through the hen's neck, severing the windpipe but not dividing it entirely. The blood was allowed to drip on the rice, which, by the way, was always *adwa* rice, or rice which had been husked without having been boiled. Then in much the same way he offered a white cock to the godlet known as Five (a group of five brothers), separating its head entirely and placing it in the second square A white hen was then offered to *Marang Buru*, and its head deposited in the third square. To *Gosae Era*, a female deity, a brown chicken was sacrificed, to *Pargana bonga* a black hen, and any sort of hens to the spirits of the deceased village headmen and the *Malik bonga*. There was another priest in the village known as the *Kudam naeke*. His special function was to offer his own blood in sacrifice, drawing it from his left forearm by pricking it with a thorn and letting it drop upon the rice.

The next step was to drive all the village cattle over the place where the sacrifices had taken place. Happy was the cow or bullock that trod upon the egg, for thereby it brought its master good luck for the coming year. In token thereof it was anointed with oil and smeared with vermilion, and its owner gave a special contribution of rice to the feast fund by way of a thank offering. For three days and three nights, dancing the *Sohrae* dance to the tune of the *Sohrae* bonga, drinking and feasting were kept up almost continuously, interspersed with indulgences of a less innocent kind. Other sacrifices were offered, and the bodies of the victims eaten. The closing act of the festival was a special distribution of rice beer to the villagers, as a sign that the licence allowed to the young men and maidens had come to an end, and that any ceremonial defilement that had been contracted during its term was now removed.

The *Sohrae* was followed by the *Sakrat*, a feast whose special feature was the dancing of the *pak don* or sword and shield dance. Since the disarmament a stick was used instead of a sword, the shield being of beaten brass and copper The young men thus equipped, and with small bells tied round their ankles, formed a circle round the drummers, and danced and capered, brandishing stick and shield, and yelled and shouted for two days, under the influence of frequent potations of rice beer. There was also a hunt, and various kinds of athletic contests in the evening. A favourite sport was to place a dozen arrows on the ground, end to end, so as to form a square or oblong. A youth squatted down, and went jumping frog-like round the arrows. Each time he completed a round without stopping to rest, he picked up an arrow, and his task was to keep up the running till all the arrows were disposed of.

Following hard after the *Sakrat* came the *Magh Sim*, a sacrifice of fowls after the reaping of the thatching grass, an operation which was regarded as the finish of the agricultural year. Then came the *Jatra*, when sacrifices having again been offered in the sacred grove, three or four of the villagers worked themselves up into a frenzy of excitement. While in this ecstatic condition they were supposed to be endowed with the gift of prophecy, and predicted the future to those who consulted them. During this time a fair was held. Traders came and erected booths for the sale of their wares, and a revolving swing was constructed, consisting of four chairs suspended between two stout uprights.

At the time of the passing of the cold weather and the first approach of the warm season, the *Baha* or flower festival was held. The villagers, on going to the grove to sacrifice, carried with them pots of water, with which, after the offerings were completed, they drenched each other. This celebration was regarded as the beginning of the *mahua* season, and feasting and merry making were now suspended for a fortnight, while the entire population devoted itself to the more serious business of gathering up the precious flowers, their manna in the wilderness, that fell like bread from heaven. All the trees within the village lands were distributed among the various householders. The sweet fleshy calyx of the flower, when ripe, fell to the ground in the early morning. Throughout the jungle the characteristic *pat pat* could be heard, and the air was heavy with the odour. Long before dawn, the people with their baskets were busily engaged gathering up the flowers. By the time the sun was well up, the bulk of the day's fall was secured; the few odd flowers that fell after that were left to the gleaners, the strangers, and the fatherless who had no trees of their own. Taking home their basketfuls, the people spread the flowers out to dry in the sun, some of it in their courtyards, and some in the threshing floors. Some they used for food at once, picking off the stamens and cooking the flowers in a pot with water till the water was boiled away. But most of it was beaten with sticks, sifted, and bound up in straw and reserved as a food supply for the working days. It was a very economical food, selling sometimes at four annas a maund and being very indigestible. "Eat a little *mahua*," the people said, "and you will not feel hungry for a long time." It was used boiled or roasted. Sometimes it was well washed in water and then taken out and roasted, and the water in which it had been washed was boiled down till it became a thick syrup. The roasted flowers were then mixed with this and eaten (rice was sometimes eaten in the same way). The well-to-do who did not depend upon the *mahua* as their food supply valued it for their cattle, or sold it to the manufactures of the distilled liquor. The fruit of the *mahua* was gathered about a month later. The kernels were split, dried, and ground, and the fine bland oil expressed from them was in general use for anointing, cooking, or lighting purposes. The rind was eaten. If unripe it was pared off, boiled, and eaten by itself or as a relish with rice. If ripe it was chewed or sucked till the juice was extracted. The fruit of the *sal* tree was gathered about the same time. It, too, was dried in the sun and then burned to separate the "feathers" or "tail." It was then split by rolling it with a board and boiled in water, which had first been mixed with wood ashes and strained. When it was softened it was taken off the fire, allowed to stand for a day, then poured out into a sieve-like basket and well washed with water. This elaborate process was necessary to get rid of the bitter astringent taste. The *sal* fruit thus prepared was often boiled and eaten mixed with *mahua* flowers.

Between the falling of the *mahua* flowers and the gathering of its fruit, the great annual hunt took place. Manka was at this time on a visit to his sister Maeno, who had married Daso Manjhi, whose home was at the foot of Parasnath Hill in the district of Hazaribagh. The hunt was a great event in that household, for Daso was *Dihri*, or Master of the Hunt, for his district of Palganj. All the hills and forests in the Santal country are divided into sections, for hunting purposes, each under the charge of a *Dihri*, whose office is hereditary. The Paresnath hunt was one of the largest, attended by thousands of men and boys. To prepare for it the jungle was burnt, to clear away the dense undergrowth Having fixed a day,—the full moon in the month of May—Daso sent round the *Dharwak*, a *sal* branch, with in this case seven leaves upon it to indicate that the gathering was due in seven days. The villagers offered sacrifices on the eve of the hunt, and on the day it was to begin Daso rose long before dawn, tied his wife's hands and feet, and laid her on a charpoy with her face towards the centre of the room. There he had deposited a vessel of water, and he told her she was to lie in the position in which he placed her, motionless and speechless, till she saw the water turn to blood. Then she could get up and go about her ordinary duties. If she did not implicitly obey this order, the hunt would be a failure. Before the sun was up she had persuaded herself that she saw the change in the water she had been told to look for, and rose with an easy mind to husk the rice.

The hunters having assembled at the foot of the hill, Daso was tied with his back to a *sal* tree and in this position performed the necessary sacrifices. Then the whole company formed into a line two or three miles long and went right through the hill, slaughtering indiscriminately everything that came in their way, to the horror of some pious Jain pilgrims who were toiling up the hill to visit the temples at the top. All had bows and arrows, and a few had old matchlock guns of Monghyr manufacture, charged with pebbles, scraps of iron, and country-made powder, with a piece of smouldering rope as tender. Manka was fortunate in bringing down a fine sambar, which he shot in the neck as it crossed his path a few yards ahead of him. The rule of the hunt was that the hind quarters belonged to him as the slayer, and the neck went to his brother-in-law as *Dihri*. A bear was also killed, a leopard was sighted but got away. Pigeons, peafowls, hares, squirrels and other small game made up the rest of the bag. In the evening the hunters feasted at the side of a stream, and then under the presidency of the *Pargana* of the district, the *Dihri*, and the village headmen, the supreme court was held at the foot of a huge banyan tree to adjudicate on all matters which were so important that they had been reserved for this gathering, and to hear appeals from the decisions of inferior bodies. It was a very democratic assembly: the opinion of the *Dihri* carried much weight in all matters pertaining to the hunt itself, and the *pargana* was the chief exponent of the law regarding everything else, but the final appeal was to the vote of the whole gathering. The proceedings lasted till midnight. A man who had married a girl of his own sept and refused to give her up had the severest sentence in the power of the court pronounced upon him. He was outcasted from the tribe and his fellow villagers were instructed to hoist a soiled leaf upon a bamboo pole opposite his house as a sign that nobody was to have any dealings with him or his. Another man who had hitherto neglected to complete his father's funeral rites was warned that if he did not speedily repair the omission a like fate would overtake him. Should Christians be outcasted? was a question argued with great warmth and animation. In some parts of the country the Christians were becoming a numerous and influential community and the attitude the others should take towards them was a matter that had to be faced. It was unanimously agreed that there could be no intermarriage between the Christians and others, but there was a good deal of difference of opinion as to whether it was permissible to eat with them or to partake of food which they had cooked. As a matter of fact, many of those present had already compromised themselves and the more conservative leaders judged it wise not to press the matter to a vote. The business being finished, the parliament adjourned to spend the interval till morning in song, music, and dance. There was a special dance, the *dunger*, danced by men alone on the night of the hunt. In the morning they retraced their steps, hunting once more over the whole hill till they reached the place from which they had started.

The hot season, too, when the tanks and rivers were at their lowest, was the fishing season. A great variety of implements were used—hooks and lines, nets and baskets, and intoxicants prepared from jungle products were often thrown into the water, to stupefy the fish and make them an easier prey.

In the matter of festivals the Santal is an eclectic. Even the too frequent festivals of his own calendar fail to satisfy him, and he appropriates his neighbours' as well. In Manka's younger days the people of Taletandi sometimes observed what they called the *pota* festival. This was simply the *Charak puja* or swinging festival of the Hindus. Hooks were fixed into the muscles of a man's back, and he was suspended from a pole which was rotated on another pole by means of ropes. Ropes were also passed under the victim's armpits to lessen the traction of the hooks. The correct thing was for the victim to fast the day before and the day following the swinging and to sleep the intervening night on thorns. Before Manka was middle-aged the custom was suppressed, but one still occasionally meets an old Santal with the marks of the hooks in the back, and in recent years attempts have been made to revive the festival, especially in times of threatened scarcity. Even when the Santals did not observe this custom themselves they sometimes hired themselves out to swing for the Hindus.

When the time for the rice sowing came round chickens were sacrificed in the sacred grove and a libation of milk was offered as well. Care was taken to sow the seed on certain auspicious days, to wit, the first three days of Rohini. Even if rain had not fallen by that time a few handfuls were sown as a matter of form. When the rice seedlings began to sprout, the demons had again to be propitiated by the sacrifice of fowls.

In July the field work began in earnest. The rice fields had been prepared beforehand by two ploughings and cleared of weeds, some of which were burned, while others were allowed to rot in water as manure; and the embankments had been repaired. Four classes of rice land were recognised,—the low, well-irrigated *baihar*; the terraced fields on the slopes above them; the upper reaches which depended entirely on the rainfall;

and the high lands where a special kind of rice was sown. When sufficient rain had fallen to work up the fields into soft, slushy mud, and the seedlings or *gachi* were about ten inches high, these were all uprooted and transplanted in little bunches of three or four. The Indian corn was sown about the same time, and the hoeing of it in the highlands alternated with the transplanting of rice in the low-lying fields.

In August the *Chhata* festival was celebrated. A bamboo umbrella was raised on the top of a pole and the people danced round it with boisterous merriment and music. Drinking and dancing continued far into the night. As the crops were ripening in the fields two more festivals were held. One was the *Karam.* The men of the village went to the jungle and cut a branch from a Karam tree (*Adina cordifolia*). This they erected in the village street, and the young folk danced round it till morning, when it was thrown into a tank. No sacrifices were offered, but a libation of liquor was poured out to the spirits of the deceased village chiefs and to *Marang Buru.* Then when the rice was turning yellow the *Janthar* was observed. Sheaves of half-ripe grain were offered in the sacred grove as the first fruits of the harvest. A pig was also sacrificed and the men ate its carcase in the grove. A similar festival was observed when the *gundli*, a small millet, began to mature.

There were other festivals as well, observed with less regularity. Of these the most important was the *jom sim*, a family sacrifice to the sun god. Well-to do families celebrated it every five years or so, and it was regarded as obligatory upon all at least once in a lifetime. It was a big affair, when cows or buffaloes were slaughtered.

There were many odd jobs, too, which filled up the intervals between the items in the above programme. Now and then Manka would burn a little lime to chew with his tobacoo. He gathered shells of fresh-water mussels or snails, put them in a broken earthen pot along with some burning cowdung, and extemporized a kiln by tying a rope to the neck of the pot and swinging it round and round. A small business was done in rearing the *tasar* silkworms on certain jungle trees and selling the cocoons. Lac and other jungle products like myrobalans were also collected and sold to traders. It was a great event in Manka's life when one of these Bengali merchants took Manka down to Calcutta with him, in charge of his goods. He had much to tell of all he had seen and heard when he returned to his village,—of houses higher than *simal* trees and ships as long as the village street—but he sacrificed his reputation for veracity altogether by declaring that he saw a river in Calcutta which was flowing one way when he crossed it in the morning, and the other way when he re-crossed it in the afternoon. That was clearly a romance of his imagination.

Old grandfather Manka had died soon after the Rebellion, and he died contented, for his eyes had beheld a great-grandson. Towards the end of the year now under review, Manka's father died of dysentery. Heavy rain had fallen in May, before the thatch of the hut had been repaired. The mud floor became a puddle and the old man contracted an illness which the alternate heat and chills, the scorchings and the drenchings, of July and August, tended to aggravate. He was very low one steamy evening in September when a raven alighted on the roof and croaked hoarsely. He was the messenger of *Jom Raj*, the King of Death, and the family concluded that its master would follow at no great interval. True enough, old Budhu died next day.

Manka had been taught to regard the proper observance of his father's funeral rites as the most sacred of all religious and social obligations. On the day of the death the corpse was carried to the river-side where a pyre was erected between four posts. The corpse was carried round the pyre three times,—perhaps with the idea of confusing the spirit and making it more difficult for it to find its way back to trouble the household,—and then deposited upon it. Manka thereupon took some cotton yarn twisted round the culm of a certain sedge and with face averted set fire to it and applied it to the mouth of the dead. The pyre was then lighted The cremation was not carried out very thoroughly and a few of the charred bones were carefully gathered up and placed in an earthen vessel. The mourners then bathed, shaved, and went home. Next day they marked out in cowdung a house for the dead, at the end of the village street, and placed some cooked rice for him within it. Some weeks later when the rains were well over and there was a break in the field work, Manka and his male relatives carried the bones they had preserved to the Damooda River—the Nai they called it. On its banks they went through the form of buying from the local Doms a small plot of land, paying as the price a couple of pice, five cowrie shells, and a little red-lead. On this piece of ground they built an altar upon which they reverently deposited the bones and prayed as follows to *Pilchu Haram* and *Pilchu Budhi*:—"Take him and lead him away. To your care we commit him." Returning home, Manka summoned all his relatives and fellow villagers to a feast called *Bhandan*. A friend supplied a cow, on the condition that when it was killed the side which first touched the ground belonged to him, the donor, the other side being devoted to the feast. There were fowls as well, and cooked rice, and rice beer, and a portion of each dish was carefully laid aside for the dead. While exceedingly scrupulous in all these observances, Manka had only very hazy and ill-defined ideas regarding the state of the dead and the future life. He believed that his father had gone to the regions where *Jom* (the Hindu *Yama*) *Raj* and *Hudul Raj* reigned, and where the departed spirits were engaged in grinding, with a pestle made from the castor-oil tree, the bones of past generations to make material for those still to be born. The only respite allowed from this toil was for mixing lime and tobacco for chewing or for nursing babies, so the men who had acquired the former habit and the women who had borne children were more fortunate than others.

CHAPTER X.

THE SEAMY SIDE.

LIFE among the Santals, even at the best, was not all beer and skittles, although they would have dearly loved to have it so; the primrose path of dalliance was strewed with thorns and it was not often or for long that Black Care vacated his seat behind the horseman. As regards physical well-being a man was fortunate if he got through the year without a single bout of fever, or if his household ever had an entirely clean bill of health. Many minor ailments, however, including parasitic skin affections, were hardly regarded as disease, because the people did not know what it was to be without them. Like heat and cold, they were part of the established order of things. The remedies, too, were sometimes worse than the ills they were meant to cure. When Manka had a headache, the result of fever, Maku took a sickle, toothed like a saw, made it red hot, and applied the entire length of its edge to his forehead and temples. When from the same cause his spleen became enlarged, a piece of rag, dipped in oil, was set on fire and placed on the skin over the organ. Once when he had toothache he went to the blacksmith, who extracted a molar with his tongs, taking with it a considerable piece of the jaw. Over Maku's and her sisters' sufferings at childbirth, when complications arose, decency compels us to draw a veil.

Then Manka and Maku lived through the great famines of 1866 and 1874 and through many other years of scarcity and anxiety. It is true they suffered less than many others, partly because poverty had always compelled them to depend upon the jungle for ekeing out their food supplies, partly because they grew a greater variety of crops than their neighbours in the rich rice lands. They never starved absolutely, because, relatively, they were always starving. When famine came, they ate not only the wild fruits, flowers, leaves and roots, which they ate at other times, but those also which as a rule only the birds and beasts devoured, and they cracked the stones of the berries and ate the kernels too. Many appeased the pangs of hunger by filling their stomachs with the earth of anthills. Some of the wild fruits they ate had curious effects, producing a state of intoxication, or causing the epidermis to peel off the body in large flakes. When the hot weather advanced and water failed, cholera added to their sufferings, but the greatest mortality took place at the beginning of the rainy season, when the famishing people, too impatient to wait for the ripening of the crops, gorged themselves with half-cooked unwholesome grain. Manka and Maku lost two of their children in an epidemic of dysentery at this time.

A public-house which was opened in the neighbourhood of Taletandi was also the source of much misery and crime. Sobriety had never been a virtue of the Santals, but their carousals of beer-drinking were usually separated by intervals of hard work and healthy exercise. But the establishment of a liquor shop in their midst opened up possibilities of habitual drunkenness that they had not dreamt of before, and some of them took full advantage thereof. "I am going on pilgrimage," a Santal would say, as he shaped his course for the publichouse, where he got gloriously drunk for four pice and was allowed to lie on a litter of straw till he was able to stagger home with bleared eyes and a splitting headache. Two friends of Manka's went one day to the bazar together, to sell a couple of ploughshares they had made. They had spent several days on the job, and they sold them for two annas each. On their way home they had to pass the public-house, where they both indulged freely. They were sober enough to resume their journey, but they took a very erratic course and nightfall found them still far from home. "Let us sleep here," said one, as they stumbled against the roots of a shady banyan tree. "No," said the other, "there are demons here; let us sleep in the open." Then they began to quarrel, till one with his heavy bamboo stick, in drunken fury, felled the other to the ground, fracturing his skull. Quite unconcerned, he lay down and slept beside the body of his victim. In the morning he realised to his dismay what he had done, but beyond throwing away his stick and washing himself and his clothes in the first stream he came to, he took no precautions to conceal his crime. He went home, and waited there till the police arrested him, when he made a full and voluntary confession. But his friends clubbed together and raised money to engage a clever lawyer, and when his trial came on he was acquitted. As usual in such cases little importance was attached to his own confession, as the facility with which the police can get confessions made to order was fully recognised.

Quarrels among the villagers were not infrequent. Manka had an old cow who had ceased to calve. Such cows were sometimes used instead of bullocks for ploughing, but there was once a riot in Taletandi when a band of Hindu pilgrims who were passing through attacked a Santal because he was ploughing with cows and nearly clubbed him to death. Manka had no scruples about the sacredness of the cow, and he thought the safest plan would be to kill this one. He offered shares to all the villagers, and the carcase was carefully divided into about thirty lots at four annas each. Some malcontents, however, declared that Manka had given his relatives and kept for himself a more generous portion than was just, and the panchayet had to meet to clear him of the charge. There were also disputes about the boundaries of fields, especially of the precious rice lands which could be slightly enlarged by taking in a few inches of the neutral embankments, and about straying cattle trespassing among the crops. In these milder cases, the village panchayet was usually able to effect a settlement, but in some graver offences its intervention unfortunately failed to keep the case out of court. A daughter of Manka's had been married to a lad in Manbhoom. A few months afterwards, she had quarrelled with her husband. He had come home tired one night from hunting and had asked her to shampoo his legs. This she refused to do, saying she was just recovering from fever, and her hands were soft. He threatened to strike her and she fled to her father's house. Other means of inducing her to return having failed, her husband brought a charge against Manka in court of having forcibly taken away his wife in order to sell her in marriage to some one else. The case came on, and Manka had to appear before the magistrate. On the court table lay a piece of tiger's skin, with tail attached. Holding the tail in his hand Manka swore, "I shall tell the whole truth and nothing but the truth; if I do not tell the truth may the tigers, the serpents, and the witches devour me." The magistrate accepted Manka's version as correct, although the great bulk of the testimony was on the other side,—for as all is fair in war, lying is allowed in litigation,—and he was acquitted. A reconciliation was affected soon afterwards, and sealed by a feast.

For years Manka's dreams were haunted by a three-legged leopard, eager to devour him. He had been cutting firewood one day in a dense part of the jungle, when looking round he saw a leopard just about to spring upon him. He ducked down, and as the brute passed over him he swung his axe with all his might and it cut one of its hind legs clean off. The leopard died, and Manka, taking up its severed leg, went through the village dangling it on a string, to the admiration of all who heard his tale. But he could not get rid of the idea that the leopard would be avenged.

In 1871, the last case of human sacrifice known to occur among the Santals took place in Manka's district. Limbu Manjhi had suffered for a long time from a painful disease and all the remedies he had tried had been of no avail. He then thought of trying the sovereign cure—the sacrifice of a human being. Such sacrifices had once been far from uncommon in that part of India, where there was at one time a regular trade in the victims used for this purpose. With the help of two other Santals and a Paharia, Limbu decoyed a stranger who was staying in his house to a lonely part of the jungle. There they seized him, gagged him, and bound him hand and foot, with his own cloth; and a small portion of his head was shaved with a razor which Limbu had brought with him for this purpose. The Paharia then did *puja*, while the others tied a creeper round the victim's neck and fastened it to a branch of a tree. The cloth was removed from his mouth as one of the party said it was not right to kill a man with his mouth closed. The two other Santals then seized the man by the legs and held him in a horizontal position while Limbu struck off his head with two blows of a sword. All were arrested. The Paharia turned informer; Limbu Manjhi was hanged, and the other two Santals transported for life.

The coolie recruiting, chiefly for labourers on the tea-gardens of Assam, was a prominent element in the social life of the Santals in the latter half of Manka's life. It provided an outlet for surplus population; it also afforded a perilously easy means by which husbands could run away with other men's wives, leaving their own behind, youths who quarrelled with their parents could play the prodigal, and debtors could escape from their creditors. The recruiters were utterly unscrupulous in their methods. Girls were decoyed away from home, or waylaid at market, drugged and outraged, and then told that they dared not return to their friends. At first, too, there was a heavy mortality among the emigrants, both in transit and on the tea-gardens, and few of those who went away were ever heard of again. The tea industry, no doubt, brought to the Santal lads the opportunity of earning money and bettering their position. But if there were chances of earning money there were also temptations to spend it; and the Santal coolie was none the less liked because, living like a lord and drinking like a fish, he squandered his wages as soon as he received them, and ere long gave up his youthful dream of saving the humble pittance that would have enabled him to return to his native village and set up as a farmer. Manka lived, however, to see most of the abuses in connection with the coolie traffic rectified,

The transport was carefully regulated, sanitary precautions were made compulsory, and the tea-planters naturally co-operated with the Government in maintaining the health and comfort of the workers who were so highly valued and sometimes so difficult to procure. One of Manka's sons became a *sirdar* in connection with a tea company in Sylhet, enlisting labourers, giving them advances of pay, and conveying them direct to the gardens without the intervention of the rapacious middleman. Another son, however, declined all the tempting offers held out to him by his *sirdar* brother, preferring to tramp up to Darjeeling and earn a little money as a free labourer. The pay was not quite so good, but he was bound by no agreement, and could strike his camp whenever the roving spirit moved him. Sometimes he took a spell of work in the coal mines near Raniganj or at Giridih.

A belief in witchcraft is one of the most devoutly cherished articles in the Santal creed. It furnishes a ready and effective weapon in social and domestic warfare. A man Ramai in Taletandi, distantly related to Manka, had married a young wife, although his first wife, by whom he had children and grand-children, was still alive and well. The young wife was good-looking and vivacious and from the day of her advent Ramai paid much less attention to the wife of his youth than to his youthful wife. Jealousy was the natural result. When two of Ramai's grand-children died, one after another, of wasting illnesses, and disease broke out among the cattle, and blight attacked a field of rice, the old wife seized the opportunity. Beyond a doubt, her young rival was a witch. She dinned this into her husband's ears; she reproached him every day and all day long for having brought such a pest into the house. She spread the same accusation among neighbours and whispered it to her children. The young woman had an evil eye—everybody could see that, the old woman said, and she had been repeatedly seen shaking her head in a way peculiar to witches, and had not a child been born blind, and a buffalo broken its leg in the village she came from? Ramai had to do something, if only to gain temporary relief from the old woman's ravings, and he resorted to the *ojha* or village medicine man. The *ojha* spent some time consulting his oracles and divining by means of *sal* leaves, and concluded that there was at least ground for suspicion. He advised Ramai to take three *sal* branches each with a different number of leaves upon it, to mark one of them as representing the suspected person, and to stick them together in a tank. If the branch that represented his junior wife withered before the others, she was clearly a witch. This particular branch did wither first, and Ramai's superstitions vanquished both his reason and his affections. He resolved to try if a good beating would exorcise the demon of witchcraft; but he and his sons fortified themselves with too much liquor, and in a frenzy of rage they dragged the unfortunate woman through the street by her hair, forced filth down her throat, and then beat her to death with solid bamboos. Everybody knew what was going on, but nobody interfered. The body was burned as quickly as possible, and the death was reported to the police as due to snake bite.

It was on a darkened stage that Manka and Maku played the final act of their life drama It is true that they were surrounded by their children and grand children, and the old home held together till the end. But old age hit them hard. As they lost their teeth they got less and less nourishment from their coarse food. When they had not vigour to work they felt the cold very keenly. It was an attack of pneumonia, the result of a wetting when she was out gathering firewood one bleak day in January, that carried Maku off. She only possessed one piece of cloth, which was soaked by the rain, and at night she wrapped herself in it and went to sleep. Manka felt his loneliness all the more, as he was now rapidly growing blind from cataract. Hs was advised to go to the Dumka Hospital or to one of the Medical Missions in neighbouring districts, but he would require some one to lead him and everybody was busy. Besides, he disliked the idea of going to live, even for a few days, in a big room with a lot of *Dikus* as he called the Hindus generally. So he placed himself in the hands of one of the itinerant *baids*, who go about the villages in India to-day, as their professional predecessors went from fair to fair in mediæval Europe, operating for cataract. Instead of removing the diseased lens, the *baid* depressed it out of its place into the interior of the eye. The immediate effect was to restore the sight, as the impediment to vision was now out of the way, but the irritation caused by the presence of the lens, dislocated from its proper place, led gradually to total blindness, not only in the eye which had been operated upon, but in the other which had until then retained a moderate amount of sight. Poor Manka could not even herd cattle now, and was dependent upon a grandchild to lead him about—and the grandchildren had all more profitable or more congenial work to do. "You must take care of the old man," a doctor once said to an old Santal woman who had brought her tottering old husband to the dispensary. "If I take care of the old man, who will take care of the pigs?" was her reply, in the reasonableness of which the old man himself acquiesed. He soon passed away but the pigs remained, as the prop of his wife's old age.

One day, not very long before the end, an English missionary pitched his camp at the end of the village street, and went from house to house, to speak to the people. It was in the cold weather. Nearly all the men were away hunting or visiting friends; the boys and girl were out in the jungle herding the cattle; and in the absence of their lords the ladies did not appear. So the only man in the village whom the missionary found to speak to was old Manka, who was sitting in the courtyard, turning his sightless eyes towards the sun and getting all the warmth he could. "*Johar*, father," said the missionary, "*Johar*, my son," said Manka, returning the Santal salutation. Then the missionary sat down and gave the old man his message. The old man listened respectfully, but shook his head. "Tell that to the young men, tell it to the village chiefs. It does not concern me. I am a rotten tree on the brink of the river. The next flood will carry me away." The missionary urged that God had spared him to hear of the true religion; had he not survived nearly all the friends and companions of his youth who had passed away without hearing of it? "Yes, I have," replied Manka, "and why should I separate myself from them now? Where they have gone, there I must follow them. Why did you not come and tell us of this sooner?" The missionary read to him and pled with him, but the old man would not move, and made no pretence of being interested.

In the end, it was cancer of the jaw that brought Manka's career to a close. The incessant chewing of tobacoo and lime was beyond a doubt the predisposing cause. It was a slow, painful death, a death in fact by starvation, for when he lost the power of eating in the natural way no one could think of any artificial method of feeding him. He welcomed death as the end of his sufferings, and his bones were duly deposited with filial care in the bed of the Damoodar River, as those of his fathers had been before him.

THE END.

Glossary.

Most of the Santali and other vernacular terms which have been used have been explained in the text. The following are a few others, which, although very familiar in India, may not be known to readers elsewhere.

Dal is the pulse, lentils or other "relish" which is eaten along with boiled rice *(bhat)*.

Dam is price.

Lota is a brass drinking vessel, varying in size from a pint to half a gallon.

Dhoti: a cloth worn round the waist, passing between the legs and fastened behind.

Chaddar means a sheet, and is used of the cloth which is worn shawl-like over the shoulders. In recent times the *Kot* (coat, or jacket) has become a common substitute for the chaddar, and "shorts" are often worn instead of the *dhoti*.

Sari is the female garment, a piece of cloth about a yard wide and anything up to six yards in length, wound round the waist and thrown over the shoulder. A *Kurta* or jacket is often worn along with it.

Doms are one of the "untouchable" tribes of India. They do scavenger work but are also in demand as musicians and dancers at marriages and other festive occasions. Dom women, often the dirtiest in the district, act as midwives.

Dhubi ghās is a common grass, *Cynodon Dactylon, Pers.*

Pies (pai) and *Pice (paisa)* must not be confused. The pie is the twelfth, and the pice a fourth, part of an anna, which is approximately a penny or the sixteenth part of a rupee.

Mahajan, literally "big man," is usually a merchant and money lender in one.

Darogha may mean the head man of any office but it is commonly used to designate the sub-inspector of police who is in charge of a *thana* or police office.

Zamindar is a landlord.

Baid is a doctor, generally one who practices one of the indigenous systems of medicine.

Ojha is used by the Santals of a witch doctor but it is a Hindi word meaning generally magician.

Sardar or *Sirdar*, also Hindi, means a chief or headman, but is most commonly used among the Santals for an overseer or an agent from the tea gardens who comes to recruit coolies.

Puja means idolatrous worship. It is Hindi; the common term among the Santals is *boṅgak'*, the verb derived from the noun *boṅga* an evil spirit.

Charpoy is a string bed or cot.

Myrobalams are the fruit of a jungle tree, *Terminalia belerica*, which is used for tanning, ink making, and other purposes.

Johar is the Santali salutation, corresponding to *Salam* among Hindi speaking people. It is also in use among some Hindu castes and is said to have been originally a war cry of the Rajputs.

The following are the principal trees fonnd in the Santal country, with their botanical names :—

Sal or *Sarjom*,	...	...	*Shorea robusta.*
Mahua or *Matkom*,	...	...	*Bassia latifolia.*
Mango, ...	...	...	*Magnifera indica.*
Jack, ...	...	...	*Artocarpus integrifolia.*
Pipal, ...	...	...	*Ficus religiosa.*
Tamarind,	...	...	*Tamarindus indica.*
Loa, ...	...	...	*Ficus glomerata.*
Banyan, ...	...	...	*Ficus bengalensis.*
Semal, cotton tree,	...	..	*Bombax heptaphyllum.*
Palas, ...	...	...	*Butea frondosa.*
Nim, ...	...	...	*Melia asad dirachta.*

Index.